THE INSTANT GOURMET

The Instant Gourmet

SOUTH BRUNSWICK AND NEW YORK:
A. S. BARNES AND COMPANY
LONDON: THOMAS YOSELOFF LTD

MIRACLE MEALS IN TEN MINUTES

F. A. Roszel

© 1971 by A. S. Barnes and Co., Inc.
Library of Congress Catalogue Card Number: 72-129183

A. S. Barnes and Co., Inc.
Cranbury, New Jersey 08512

Thomas Yoseloff Ltd
108 New Bond Street
London W1Y OQX, England

ISBN 0-498-07791-8
Printed in the United States of America

Contents

Acknowledgments 7

Introduction 9

English Equivalent Measures 10

1. Scandwiches 13
   These topless delights are the "now" thing for entertaining or for feeding a family. Dainty, nourishing, and tasty, they are also easy to prepare. While holding calories to a reasonable level, they are tops in taste and gourmet fare.

2. Casseroles 32
   The oven does the work while you engage in other pursuits, like meditating thoughtfully over a chilled glass of your favorite cooking wine!

3. That Jiffy Electric Skillet 46
   Also called an electric frying pan, for a snack or a meal this appliance is an aid to no-work meal preparation. Here's the know-how for the swinging chef.

4. Tricks with Instant Potatoes 60
   No more problems with storing, peeling, and mashing the Irish fruit. When you know the tricks, gourmet potato dishes are a breeze. The instants are delightful in a wide variety of dishes from soups through entrees and pastry.

5. Quick Stunts with Sausage   70

All the tricks and recipes for quick preparation of dishes with the versatile and tasty porkies.

6. Blender Specialties   82

This no-nonsense tool of the Instant Gourmet turns the clock 'way back on the kitchen game. It saves hours of tedious chopping, pureeing, mixing, crumbing, and grinding. Fantastic soups, sauces, and gravies are easy with its quick-as-a-wink handling of otherwise difficult problems in fast food preparation—from baby foods to beverages, pancakes and waffles, and entrees hot and cold. All the recipes and tricks for "right-now" meals with the flick of a switch.

7. Suddenly French   164

Everyone dreams of being a French gourmet chef. French cooking is a mood—and need not be at all tedious. Here are the secrets of French cookery—wine, brandy, sauce, and decoration—from hors d'oeuvres to desserts à la mode.

8. Party Cooking with Wine   202

Wine is joy—and taste beyond belief. Give a wine party, with wine tasting, wine cooking, and maybe a little wine drinking. The selection, storing, serving, and cooking with wine.

9. The Art of Seasoning   214

The rules for getting the tastes of the great chefs into your favorite dishes. These skills can make your fame as a chef.

Index   219

Acknowledgments

In offering these aids to the instant gourmet, the author must gratefully share credit with the great J. H. Breland of the Isaac Delgado School of Commercial Cookery in New Orleans, whose firm grounding in the preparation of fine foods has helped me materially.

A full measure of credit must also go to the Institute of Food Chemistry of the University of Illinois, for training in the use of modern ingredients to produce tasty, nutritionally balanced meals. This has been of immeasurable value in my years of serving the discerning public.

Introduction

The day of the instant gourmet chef is here. Today (or at the latest, tomorrow) you can serve instant gourmet meals with almost a flick of the wrist. Think of it, no more tedious preparation in the kitchen while your guests get "sloshed" waiting for the results of your toil.

You can now show up cool, calm, and collected—and join your guests in a gourmet dinner that has been prepared with your own new-skilled pinkies—with not a hair out of place. You won't even have to repair your make-up!

The recipes and methods presented here in this labor-saving revelation will enable you to make eye-tempting and taste-exciting dishes, using all the modern instant ingredients, methods, and shortcuts. You will build a reputation as a gourmet chef, and no one will suspect that you didn't spend long hours in the preparation of the delights you serve.

ENGLISH EQUIVALENT
Measures

	American	English
1 cup of breadcrumbs (fresh)	1½ oz.	3 oz.
1 cup of flour or other powdered grains	4 oz.	5 oz.
1 cup of sugar	7 oz.	8 oz.
1 cup of icing sugar	4½ oz.	5 oz.
1 cup of butter or other fats	8 oz.	8 oz.
1 cup of raisins, etc.	5 oz.	6 oz.
1 cup of grated cheese	4 oz.	4 oz.
1 cup of syrup, etc.	12 oz.	14 oz.

1 English pint	20 fluid ounces
1 American pint	16 fluid ounces
1 American cup	8 fluid ounces
8 American tablespoons	4 fluid ounces
1 American tablespoon	½ fluid ounce
3 American teaspoons	½ fluid ounce
1 English tablespoon	⅔ to 1 fluid ounce (approx.)
1 English tablespoon	4 teaspoons

The American measuring tablespoon holds ¼ oz. flour.

THE INSTANT GOURMET

1. Scandwiches

When it comes to sudden food preparation, the Scandinavians are no slouches. The art of making *Smorrebrod,* as these topless sandwiches are known in Denmark, is a specialty of the Scandinavian countries. We call them "Scandwiches," and this denotes a topless sandwich with plenty of middle.

Since bread is the foundation of all topless sandwiches, the Danes argue, reasonably enough, that with a sandwich, as with a house, all you need is one foundation. Who would think of putting a second foundation on top of a beautiful house? History does not reveal whether or not the Earl of Sandwich was only trying to top the Danes when he put a second slice of bread on top of his sandwich.

Be the origin what it may, a Scandwich is an eye-filling delight that does not over-fill the diner.

AIDS TO THE SCANDWICH CHEF

To construct a Scandwich, you must start with a slice of bread (usually buttered) as foundation. With the many kinds of breads available today, you can introduce great variety of taste and color to your foundations.

The true art in making these little culinary masterpieces lies in the imagination of the host, or hostess, making them. The possible blends of color and taste are endless, and you can please both the palate and the eye at the same time. Small ones make delightful hors d'oeuvres, and the tall ones are almost a full meal, with their variety of ingredients stacked high above the base.

We admit it would be helpful if some clever chef could invent edible paper clips to hold the almost flower-like arrangement of thin slices of this and that together.

In eating Scandwiches, you do not pick them up. Using a knife and fork, you slice down through the whole mélange, which results in your being able to pick up a lot of delicate bits from the ensuing wreckage. You can take comfort in knowing that leaving off the top, while it makes handling a little more difficult, has given you a substantial bonus in reduced starch intake.

Scandwich construction lends itself to adding layers of sliced and spreadable edibles in various combinations. Lobster paste, liverwurst, smoked meat pâté, deviled ham, and salmon—along with a wide variety of other spreads—are available. You can really let your imagination rove free in designing these combinations. The tremendous selection of sliceables in the meat and cheese areas gives you additional latitude in putting rolled and folded combinations into the stack.

The following recipes and directions will serve as a guideline for making these delectable Scandwiches and will stimulate your imagination into flights of fancy in creating many more toothsome delights. Under the name "Danwiches" they are sweeping the world of eating and entertainment.

Scandwiches

SCANDWICH TOPPINGS AND SAUCES

Finely diced chicken in lime jelly, chopped coarsely, makes a colorful topping with a good tang.

Red Meat Jelly—for dicing and topping
Dissolve beef or chicken bouillon cube in a half pint of boiling water. Soften one envelope of gelatin in ½ cup cold water. Add to hot bouillon and stir. Add a dash of Worcestershire sauce and 1 teaspoon lemon juice. Let set, then dice and use as a tasty, colorful topping.

Fleurette Salad (great with cold bacon or pork)
½ cup tiny cauliflower flowerets, blanched one minute in boiling water, then drained and cooled quickly.
½ cup sliced button mushrooms
3 tbsps. grated carrot
1 tsp. lemon juice
¼ cup frozen peas, cooked one minute, drained, and chilled.
3 tbsps. mayonnaise

Beet Salad
¼ cup finely diced beets (cooked)
1 finely chopped gherkin
¼ cup lightly cooked green peas
1 celery stalk, and tender leaves, finely chopped
1 tsp. lemon juice
¼ tsp. sugar
4 tbsps. mayonnaise
   Toss together lightly and serve where called for.

Sudden Remoulade Sauce
½ cup mayonnaise

2 tbsps. finely chopped mixed pickles (sweet)
1 tbsp. prepared mustard

Curry Mayonnaise (wonderful with hard-boiled eggs, fish, and cold meats)
½ cup mayonnaise
¼ tsp. Worcestershire sauce
1 tsp. curry powder
1 tsp. lemon juice
½ tsp. sugar
dash of cayenne

Horseradish Cream
3 ozs. cream cheese
¼ cup whipping cream
2 tbsps. horseradish
1 tsp. lemon juice
1 egg white beaten stiff
¼ tsp. salt (dash Tabasco if desired)
   Cream the cream and cream cheese and add lemon juice and horseradish. Fold in beaten egg white.

Here are a number of easy-to-prepare spoon-on toppings and dressings that add taste and color to the Scandwich.

Cucumber and onion
Remove the seedy center from the cucumber and dice finely. Slice an onion thinly and dice finely. Put both together in a bowl and coat well with two tablespoons salt. Let stand an hour and then wash off all the salt, soaking a few minutes before draining. Sprinkle with one tablespoon lemon juice, then toss with mayonnaise. The salt treatment removes the heat from the onions and the burp from the cucumbers, so you can remain

friends with your guests. A spoonful of this mixture on meats such as liver pâté or chicken loaf adds a zing of flavor.

Fried Apple Slices
Fried lightly in bacon fat, these slices are a tasty item to include with the toppings on pork products.

Hamlet Salad Topping
3 tbsps. mayonnaise
1 tbsp. chopped sweet gherkins
2 tbsps. diced pickled beets
4 tbsps. diced lunchmeat of your choice

Ceylon Salad
8 tbsps. mayonnaise
1 tsp. curry powder
¼ tsp. Worcestershire sauce
2 tbsps. chopped anchovies
4 tbsps. chopped hard-boiled egg

Nelson Salad
2 tbsps. mayonnaise
1 tsp. lemon juice
½ tsp. sugar
4 tbsps. mixed cooked carrots and peas
1 tbsp. chopped parsley or chives
1 tbsp. chopped watercress
   Toss together and let stand an hour to develop flavor.

Egg Strips
2 eggs
2 tbsps. milk
¼ tsp. salt

⅛ tsp. savory
pinch of black pepper

Beat all ingredients together. Pour into greased shallow pan and bake in 300° oven until firm. Sprinkle part with paprika and part with chopped parsley or chives. Cut in strips to use as topping or garnish.

GARNISHES FOR SCANDWICHES

Part of the joy of making Scandwiches is the variety of things you can use to enhance taste and appearance: little sticks made of green pepper and raw carrot, tiny gherkins, chopped chives or chopped shallot tops, fried apple slices, fried and raw onion rings, sliced stuffed olives, raw tomato wedges, asparagus tips, carrot curls, sliced hard-boiled eggs, radish roses, leaf lettuce, curly endive, watercress, and parsley sprigs. All, in the proper combination, add piquancy and eye-appeal to the finished product. Pleasing the eye is a desirable start for pleasing the palate.

Preparation of toppings and garnishes is important for giving a lush appearance to the edibles. In preparing gherkins or small dills, slice thinly lengthwise almost to the end, then spread into a fan. Slice cucumbers, oranges, or tomatoes, then cut two thirds of the way across the slice and twist the two halves in opposite direction for a butterfly effect.

To add height and beauty to the toppings, partly roll each thin slice of meat and stack in threes. Each roll rests on the unrolled part of the preceding slice. On the last roll, a pickle fan, tomato wedges, asparagus tips, capers, or mushroom slices will finish out the effect. Slices of bacon, rolled and secured with a toothpick and then grilled, make tasty and attractive morsels in topping.

Buttering the bread well prevents dressings from penetrating into it and making it soggy; no one loves a soggy sandwich.

SUGGESTED SCANDWICH PARTY
SHOPPING LIST
(For Twelve)

Breads
1 loaf rye, dark or light
1 loaf whole wheat
1 white sandwich loaf
pumpernickel, corn breads, or other breads of your choice are also good

Cheeses
½ lb. each of Samsoe, Tilsit, Cheshire, or other cheeses such as Esrom, Danablu, Gouda, hickory-smoked, wine-cured, etc.

Meats
¼ lb. sliced salami (not too garlicky!)
½ lb. sliced chicken loaf
¼ lb. thinly sliced corned beef
½ lb. lean bacon slices
½ lb. liverwurst loaf, sliced, *or*
½ lb. liver and bacon loaf
1 can (about 6 ozs.) deviled ham

Other Ingredients
1 can sliced pickled beets
1 jar sweet pickled gherkins
1 or 2 medium-sized dill pickles
1 large cucumber
1 orange
1 lemon
1 lb. firm red tomatoes
1 head lettuce
1 bunch parsley
1 bunch watercress
1 lb. butter
1 can diced carrots
1 can small peas
1 can button mushrooms
2 large mild onions
1 small can pimentos, for color strips.

When selecting cheeses you should pay attention to the make-up of your party, as to the proportion of male to female. Most men prefer stronger cheeses than women. The same holds true of cheese spreads. Most men prefer horseradish cheese spread to the milder chive flavor preferred by most women.

This shopping list is intended only as a guide. With a little experience in making Scandwiches, you can use your imagination in designing and building your masterpieces.

The Elsinore
This one leads to dreams of Copenhagen's Tivoli Gardens —or maybe *Midsummer's Night* at the witching hour. This is a gay and mouth-watering tribute to Denmark.

The What
4 slices hard-boiled egg
½ oz. black caviar
½ oz. mayonnaise
4 slices tomato
lettuce
dark rye or pumpernickel bread

The How
Butter the bread. Place on a lettuce leaf a little larger than the bread slice. Arrange egg and tomato slices in two lines, side by side. Pipe mayonnaise down the middle of the lines and then spoon caviar on top of the line of mayonnaise. It looks exotic—and is.

Curly Top
They'll ask for more of this saucy Scandwich.

The What
3 slices pork luncheon meat, loaf size, *or*
4 slices canned luncheon meat of your choice.
2 cooked prunes, stoned
lettuce
parsley
buttered sandwich bread, toasted or plain
1 tbsp. horseradish cream (See spoon-on toppings)
1 slice fresh orange

The How
Fold the meat slices, one in front of the other, on the bread. Spoon the horseradish cream onto center. Cut orange slice and twist. Place over the cream in a twist and place prunes on either side.

Fairy Tale
So named for Hans Christian Anderson, here is a simple and delightful version.

The What
1 large or several small slices liverwurst or pâté loaf
1 slice buttered rye bread
6 slices butter-fried mushrooms
1 gherkin
1 tomato slice
1 lettuce leaf
1 large slice crisp bacon

The How
Pâté should be chilled in order to slice easily. Butter the bread and cover with liverwurst or pâté. Slice and fan the gherkin. Pile on the mushroom slices, place the gherkin fan to one side of mushrooms, and lay the bacon across. Garnish with twisted slice of tomato. Tuck a little lettuce under the twist for extra color.

The Yorkshire
Britons and Norsemen, due to their history, share many common tastes. Good rare roast beef is one, and you will certainly enjoy it with this garnish of grated horseradish, remoulade sauce, and gherkin fan.

The What
2 slices rare roast beef
1 tbsp. remoulade sauce
2 tbsps. golden fried onion
1 slice tomato
1 lettuce leaf

1 gherkin, cut into a fan
1 tsp. grated horseradish
1 slice white or brown bread, buttered

The How
Arrange slices of beef on bread. Put on, side-by-side the onions, remoulade sauce and lettuce. Add tomato twist on top and lay a gherkin beside it. Good fare for lusty eaters.

Odin's Joy
Wherever you meet a Dane, at some point he will be eating roast pork and red cabbage. This is naturally a favorite among Norsemen or their descendents.

The What
2 slices cold roast pork
2 tbsps. pickled red cabbage
1 prune
1 orange slice
1 slice dark rye bread, buttered
1 small piece of lettuce

The How
Arrange the pork slices to overlap sides of bread, in a circle if possible. Mound the red cabbage in the center and crown it with a twisted orange slice. Tuck a small piece of lettuce and a stoned prune on opposite sides of the twist.

Farm Picnic
Bacon goes with egg like girl with boy. This substantial Scandwich is a real hunger-queller.

The What
6 slices hard-boiled egg
2 slices fried lean bacon
1 slice tomato
1 lettuce leaf
1 sprig watercress
1 slice rye or wheat bread, buttered

The How
Arrange lettuce leaf overlapping one end of bread. Put on egg slices, overlapping in two rows. Place the bacon slices side by side along the rows of egg slices. Twist the tomato slice on top of bacon and tuck sprig of cress into the twist.

Carissima
Of all good spicy sausages, salami is considered king. Those with little or no garlic are best for Scandwiches.

The What
4 thin slices large salami
4 thin slices mild onion
small leaf of green lettuce
1 large sprig parsley
1 slice buttered rye bread

The How
Press lettuce into butter on one corner of bread. Fold salami slices loosely in half and stack on bread. Put onion rings on top. Tuck the parsley sprig into corner where lettuce is. Sprinkle paprika on onion rings for color.

The Goddess
Maybe also food for the Gods; tasty and filling.

The What
1 medium-sized fried drumstick, or quarter of frying chicken
1 slice lean bacon, soft fried and rolled
2 slices cucumber
1 slice tomato
1 lettuce leaf
1 sprig watercress
buttered white bread

The How
Arrange lettuce leaf to cover the bread. Put quarter chicken or drumstick on top. (*Note:* wrap end of drumstick in aluminum foil.) Put tomato slice between two slices cucumber. Cut and twist, then place on top of chicken. Tuck in the bacon roll and a sprig of watercress.

The Skagway International
This has an impressive name, and an equally impressive flavor.

The What
2 slices cooked ham
2 dessertspoons Beet Salad (see Toppings)
1 tomato slice
2 cucumber slices
lettuce
1 sprig parsley
1 slice pumpernickel, buttered

The How
Fold the meat slices and arrange on the bread so the

folds will add height. Place a small piece of lettuce on top. Spoon on salad. Put tomato slice between cucumber slices. Cut and twist, then put on top of salad. Tuck sprig of parsley into one side of the twist.

Chef's Favorite
I suggest this is so named because it is easy to make, colorful, and tasty.

The What
3 slices cooked ham
2 slices tomato
1 slice cucumber
1 egg strip
1 level tsp. chopped chives
buttered white bread

The How
Arrange the slices of ham around the bread with overlaps in the center. Place egg strip across center. Put the cucumber slice between two firm slices of tomato, all about equal size. Cut two thirds of the way across the slices and twist in opposite directions. Place straddling the egg strip and add some chives.

The Gulf Coast
Small peeled shrimp are the *pièce de résistance* of this toothsome Scandwich.

The What
2 ozs. shrimp, fresh cooked, canned or frozen
1 heaping tbsp. mayonnaise
1 slice lemon, or 2 wedges

1 sprig parsley or watercress
2 slices tomato, cubed
1 long slice bread (These high loaves are available at bakeries or delicatessens.)

The How
Butter bread and cover with lettuce. Pipe a line of mayonnaise (or rosettes of mayonnaise) and press three lines of shrimp along length of bread. (If shrimp are larger use two lines.) Sprinkle tomato cubes on and add more mayonnaise. Place twisted lemon slice on one end and tuck in parsley or cress.

The Sea Breeze
The Scandinavians fish for and love herring, so it is inevitable that they would use them in a Scandwich.

The What
3 slices pickled herring
3 onion rings
parsley sprig
1 tomato wedge
lettuce
1 slice buttered rye bread

The How
Press a piece of lettuce into butter on one corner of the Scandwich. Cut herring into strips and place diagonally on bread. Put on the onion rings, overlapping across the top and tuck a tomato wedge and parsley sprig into the lettuce corner.

King Neptune
Served hot or cold on a Scandwich, fried filet of sole,

plaice, or haddock is delicious. For easy preparation one of the Shake and Bake type coatings can be used.

The What
1 fried fish fillet of your choice
1 tbsp remoulade sauce
1 lemon slice
crisp lettuce leaf
1 sprig watercress
¼ slice tomato
1 slice buttered bread

The How
Place the fish fillet on a generous lettuce leaf and place on bread. Spoon remoulade sauce onto fish. Twist the lemon slice on the sauce. Tuck in the sprig of cress and top it with the tomato. On Friday or any other day, this Scandwich is delicious.

The Farmer's Choice
This colorful and tasty cheese Scandwich is a favorite at snacktime or mealtime.

The What
2 sticks tilsit, samsoe, or cheddar cheese
3 slices tomato
1 lettuce leaf
1 slice buttered bread
1 pinch celery salt

The How
Place the lettuce leaf and overlapping tomato slices on

the bread. Arrange the cheese sticks on top in the form of a V. Sprinkle with celery salt or paprika.

Blue Danube
Many people love the piquant flavor of Danish blue cheese. If you are among those who do, this Scandwich will delight your palate.

The What
3 slices Danablu or Mycella cheese
1 small lettuce leaf
2 halves black grapes or black olives
1 slice pumpernickel bread, buttered

The How
Press the lettuce leaf into butter at one end of bread. Overlap the cheese slices on top. Lay the grape or olive halves at the joins in the slices. As the French say, *tres piquante*, especially if they use Camembert or Gorgonzola cheese.

The Geneva
Farm cheeses such as Havarti, mild cheddar, and Tilsit are a favorite for making Scandwiches.

The What
1 long slice lean bacon, cut in two and fried
2 slices Havarti, Tilsit, or cheddar
2 tbsps. coarsely chopped watercress
¼ tomato, wedge shape
1 small lettuce leaf
1 large slice french bread, buttered

The How
Cut the cheese slices in two. Place one of the slices on the bread, and then the leaf of lettuce only half covering the cheese. Then arrange a slice of cheese and a slice of bacon, all overlapping slightly. Repeat with another slice of cheese, another slice of bacon, and the remaining half slice of cheese. Top with the watercress and tomato quarter.

The Tempter
This Scandwich blends the flavor of spiced pork loaf with mild cheese and a touch of dill—a fortunate blend, indeed.

The What
2 slices Esrom, Gouda, or other cheese
1 slice spiced pork loaf
3 thin slices dill pickle, sliced lengthwise
1 lettuce small leaf
1 stuffed olive, sliced
1 slice buttered bread

The How
Tuck the lettuce leaf into the butter on one corner of the bread. Cut the spiced pork slice in two. Now, in overlapping layers, put on a slice of pork, then cheese, pork, and cheese. Lay stuffed olive slices on top of each slice.

Other Suggestions for Scandwich Fillings

Salami with slices of headcheese and chopped chives.
Salami or pork roll slices filled with horseradish cream, rolled, and garnished with stuffed olives.

Scandwiches

Ham slice with pineapple slice and chive cream cheese.

Cocktail sausages and bacon rolls on lettuce with sliced boiled new potatoes, mayonnaise, chopped parsley, and tomato splinter.

Franks or Vienna sausages coarsely chopped and mounded with new potato and onion salad.

Chopped pork and ham, potato, mayonnaise, watercress, and radish roses.

Roast sliced chicken on cress with tomato cubes.

Hard-boiled egg slices with anchovy fillets and slices of stuffed olive.

Cod's roe (canned or smoked) on lettuce with lemon twist.

Tuna fish on lettuce with mayonnaise or horseradish cream, lemon twist, and cress.

Fried soft roe on lettuce with raw onion rings and chopped bacon.

Apple slices with bacon strips and tomato splinters.

Camembert cheese with Mandarin orange slices.

Mild cheddar cheese with chutney and chopped aspic.

Danish blue cheese with shredded carrot and black grape halves.

Canned corned beef and cucumber and onion slices.

Sliced pepperoni, sliced green pepper rings, mozzarella cheese, and tomato cubes.

2. Casseroles

The invention of the casserole has been a great aid to the cook in a hurry. With one main dish and a side dish of salad, you have it made.

Salmon Noodle Casserole
This casserole is fish in one of its most attractive forms. Even those children who are not too wild about eating fish will love it!

The What
1 package (4½ ozs.) regular size noodles
1½ cups milk
1 can (7 ozs.) tuna or salmon, drained and flaked
1 cup frozen green peas
1 envelope cream of mushroom soup mix
1 tbsp. parsley flakes
½ tsp. tarragon flakes
⅛ tsp. black pepper
¾ cup bread crumbs
3 tbsps. butter or margarine

Casseroles

The How
Cook noodles according to package directions. Heat milk, but do not boil. Stir in the soup mix and stir-cook until smooth and thick, but do not boil. Put noodles into a 1½-quart casserole. Mix in the sauce, fish, peas, and seasonings. Toss breadcrumbs in the melted butter and top casserole with them. Bake uncovered for 25 to 30 minutes in a 350° oven. For a variation in flavor, mix ½ cup of crumbled, crisp bacon with the crumbs. *Serves 4 to 6.*

Creamy Beany Casserole
The What
1 cup diced bacon, sliced franks, or leftover roast
1 10-oz. pkg. frozen French-style green beans
1 envelope cream of mushroom soup mix
1½ cups milk
¼ tsp. thyme or savory
½ cup buttered bread crumbs

The How
Cook beans according to package directions and drain well. Heat milk in saucepan and stir in soup mix. Stir below boil until sauce thickens. Add meat, beans, and seasonings and put in casserole. Top with buttered crumbs and bake at 350° for 20 to 25 minutes.

Lobster 'n Rice Casserole
The What
2 5-oz. cans lobster meat
2 tbsps. butter or bacon fat
2 tbsps. medium-dry sherry
½ tsp. paprika

1 envelope cream of mushroom soup mix
1 cup liquid from lobster (add milk to make 1 cup if necessary)
1 cup heavy cream
½ tsp. tarragon flakes

The How
Cut up lobster into bite size chunks. Saute in the butter for 3 minutes, turning and stirring. Sprinkle with the tarragon flakes and the paprika. Remove from heat. In another pan, stir soup mix into milk and juice and bring to a boil. Stir-cook until thickened and then stir in cream and sherry. Cook until quite thick and pour over lobster. *Serves 4 to 6.*

Mixed Vegetable Casserole
The What
1 pkg. frozen lima beans
1 pkg. frozen peas
1 pkg. frozen cut green beans
¾ cup dairy sour cream
¼ cup mayonnaise
⅓ cup grated Parmesan cheese
¼ tsp. salt
paprika

The How
Put frozen limas in 1 quart boiling salted water and boil five minutes. Add beans and boil 5 minutes more. Add peas and boil 2 minutes more. Drain well. Mix in mayonnaise and sour cream. Put in 2-quart casserole. Sprinkle with salt, cheese, and paprika. Bake in 325° oven 20 to 25 minutes.

Calico Casserole Beans
The What
2 cans (1 lb.) pork and beans
1 tbsp. green pepper flakes
2 tbsps. onion flakes
¼ tsp. garlic salt
2 tsps. dill flakes
2 tbsps. French mustard
2 tbsps. brown sugar
6 frankfurters, split

The How
Mix all ingredients except franks in casserole. Brush franks with mustard and place on top. Bake 30 minutes at 350°.

Fast Cheese 'n Rice Casserole
The What
1 cup chopped onion *or*
4 tbsps. instant onion flakes
1 cup uncooked rice
2 cups canned tomatoes
1½ cups water
4 chicken bouillon cubes
½ tsp. oregano flakes
¼ tsp. pepper
½ tsp. paprika
¼ lb. butter or margarine
8 slices strong process cheese, or sliced cheddar

The How
Cook onion in butter until soft. Add rice and cook until golden in color. Add balance of ingredients except cheese.

Bring to a boil and stir until bouillon cubes dissolve. In a 1½-quart casserole put a layer of rice, using ⅓ of rice. Cut 6 slices of cheese in thin strips and place ⅓ of the strips on the layer of rice. Repeat until rice and cheese strips are all used. Bake covered at 350° for 50 to 55 minutes. Cut remaining cheese in strips and add to top of rice. Sprinkle with paprika and bake uncovered five to seven minutes until cheese is melted.

Burgerole
A favorite with children of any age—even 40 or over!

The What
1 lb. ground beef
¼ cup chopped, or 2 tbsps. instant minced, onion
½ tsp. salt
½ tsp. marjoram (or savory)
1 8-oz. can tomato sauce
¼ cup chili sauce (or ketchup)
¼ tsp. pepper
8 slices strong process cheese
1 can refrigerated dinner rolls

The How
Cook meat and onion with seasonings until lightly browned. Stir in tomato and chili sauces. Put a layer of meat mix into a 2-quart casserole, and then add strips of cheese slices. Alternate layers and top with cheese. Place dinner rolls around rim of casserole and bake 20 to 25 minutes at 400° until golden. To serve, split rolls and fill with meat mixture, or any other way that makes your diners happy.

Indian Casserole
Rice n' stuff at its most edible stage.

The What
¼ cup butter
1 cup uncooked rice
1 tsp. onion flakes
2 cups cubed ham or pork, cooked
2⅔ cups water
¼ cup coarsely chopped nuts
½ cup golden raisins
1 envelope chicken rice soup mix
⅛ tsp. cinnamon
⅛ tsp. clove

The How
Sauté ham and rice in butter until rice is golden in color. Mix well in a 2-quart casserole with balance of ingredients. Bake covered at 375° for 25 minutes. Stir and bake uncovered at 350° for 10 minutes more. Serve with a salad and Roquefort dressing.

Turkey Casserole
This is a beautiful solution to the problem of leftover turkey. Slice what you can and save the small chunks for soup or hash, or you can even mix them into the stuffing.

The What
3 cups sliced cooked turkey
1 can baby clams (10½ oz.), drain and save liquid
⅓ cup butter or margarine

3 tbsps. instant minced onion (or flakes)
5 slices toast, diced
1 tbsp. parsley flakes
1 tsp. salt
½ tsp. thyme
1 beaten egg
¼ tsp. paprika
4 tbsps. celery flakes

The How
Heat the butter, add seasonings, vegetable flakes, toast cubes, and clams, and stir in egg. Add ⅓ cup of clam juice, and more if required to moisten stuffing. Spread one third of stuffing in bottom of casserole. Add a layer of turkey, a layer of stuffing, and the balance of turkey. Top with stuffing. Bake covered at 350° for 20 minutes, uncovered for 10 minutes. If a sauce is desired, a good one is made with 1 can mushroom soup, ½ cup condensed milk, 3 tablespoons sherry, and 1 tablespoon parsley flakes. Heat and serve as a side gravy or sauce.

Casserole Shepherd Pie
Most people will love the flavor and goodness of this recipe. Several kinds of leftover meat can be used, if you wish.

The What
2½ cups cubed or ground cooked meat
1 tbsp. flour
2 tbsps. onion flakes
2 tbsps. oil or bacon fat
2½ cups gravy, canned or homemade
6 or 8 small onions, canned
1 can mixed carrots and peas, or 1 small can of each

Casseroles

⅛ tsp. sage
½ tsp. thyme
1 egg, beaten
1 can consommé
3 cups mashed potatoes, or instant
salt and pepper to taste

The How
Coat the meat with flour and brown lightly in fat. Add gravy, vegetables, onion flakes and seasonings and heat through. Place in casserole. In preparing topping, mash the potatoes with as much consommé as required for desired texture. Fold in the egg and drop by spoonfuls in circles on top of meat mixture. (If preparing instant mashed potatoes, use consommé instead of the water and milk called for.) Bake at 425° for about 25 minutes until potatoes are golden peaks. *Serves 4 or 5.*

Savory Pork Casserole
This is a true family meal, country style.

The What
2 lbs. pork chops, cut for number of servings required
3 tbsps. flour
1 tsp. salt
½ tsp. cumin seed
⅛ tsp. sage
8 medium sized potatoes
hot milk
2 apple halves

The How
Trim off excess fat from pork and melt in frying pan. Mix the seasonings with flour and coat the chops. Brown

in the melted fat and transfer to casserole. Halve the potatoes (scrubbed or peeled) and place around meat. Mix any seasoned flour left over with hot milk, enough to cover potatoes and apple halves. Bake uncovered at 350° for 50 to 60 minutes. *Serves up to 6.*

Fish Stick Medley
Four minutes for you—40 for the oven!

The What
1 8-oz pkg. frozen fish sticks, thawed
1 10-oz. pkg. frozen mixed vegetables, partly thawed
1 tsp. salt
2 tbsps. sherry, or 1 tbsp. lemon juice
2 tbsps. butter or margarine
1 8-oz. can tomato sauce
½ tsp. tarragon flakes

The How
While oven heats to 350°, spread the vegetables in bottom of casserole. Sprinkle with salt and pepper and dot with butter. Pour tomato sauce over and lay fish sticks on top. Sprinkle with tarragon and sherry or lemon juice. Bake uncovered for 40 minutes.

Canadian Cheese 'n Bacon
The beautiful back bacon adds flavor excellence.

The What
2 10-oz. pkgs. frozen broccoli, cooked
1 4-oz. can sliced mushrooms, drained
milk, added to mushroom liquid to make 1 cup
1 1½-oz. envelope cheese sauce mix

10 ¼" slices back bacon
½ tsp. basil

The How
While oven is heating to 375°, cook the broccoli as directed on package. Combine milk and cheese sauce mix. Cook until thickened. Place broccoli in casserole and sprinkle with basil. Pour on cheese sauce. Top with bacon slices and bake for 25 minutes, uncovered.

Spud and Cheese Casserole
This is tasty, hearty, and oh so filling.

The What
2 tbsps. melted butter
2 eggs, beaten
2 cups milk
½ tsp. salt
¼ tsp. pepper
1 cup grated cheddar cheese, *mixed with*
1 cup crumbled cooked bacon *and*
2 tbsps. chopped chives, or flakes
5 large potatoes, sliced thin

The How
Put melted butter in casserole. Put in layer of potatoes and sprinkle with cheese-bacon-chive mixture. Repeat until ingredients are all used. Pour milk, mixed with seasonings, over top. Bake at 350° for 40 to 45 minutes until potatoes are tender.

Tummy Picnic Casserole
Great at home, in the garden, or on picnic (heated on the barbecue).

The What
4 large potatoes, sliced thin
1 large onion, chopped
1½ cups consommé
¼ cup chili sauce
½ tsp. curry powder
2 eggs, beaten
1 tsp. salt
¼ tsp. pepper
1 cup mild cheddar cheese, diced
2 tbsps. butter
1 tbsp. flour
8 large frankfurters, viennas, or cooked sausage

The How
Melt butter in casserole. Add layer of potatoes, then cheese, and continue until used up. Top with onions. Mix consommé, beaten eggs, seasonings, and flour. Pour over, and bake covered for 50 minutes at 350°. Uncover, put sliced wieners, franks, or sausage on top. Cook uncovered 15 minutes before serving.

Casserole Onion Custard
This creamy, feathery onion custard is a delight with chicken, turkey, seafood, or veal.

The What
¼ cup butter or margarine
6 medium onions, sliced and chopped
2 eggs, beaten
1 cup milk
½ tsp. paprika

1 tsp. salt
⅛ tsp. pepper
¼ tsp. nutmeg or curry powder

The How
Melt butter in saucepan and sauté onions slowly until golden. Stir frequently. Combine remaining ingredients, add onions, and pour into buttered casserole. Sprinkle with paprika or parsley flakes. Bake uncovered for 25 to 30 minutes at 375° until custard is set. *Serves 6.*

Egg and Onion Casserole
You can prepare this one ahead, refrigerate, then reheat when required.

The What
2 large onions, sliced thin
2 tbsps. butter
1 tbsp. softened butter
3 tbsps. flour
1 cup grated cheese
1½ cups milk
4 hard-boiled eggs, sliced
1 tbsp. parsley or green pepper flakes
½ tsp. salt
¼ tsp. pepper

The How
Fry onions slowly in butter, without browning, over low heat until soft. Work flour into soft butter and stir into milk. Cook with onions until sauce begins to thicken. Add cheese, seasonings, and parsley or pepper flakes. Stir

and cook until cheese is well melted and combined. Put egg slices in casserole, pour in sauce, and bake for 25 minutes, uncovered at 350°. *Serves 4.*

Chicken Breasts Vladimir
We don't know for sure who Vladimir was, but his cheffing is certainly one of the goodies to remember.

The What
4 halves of chicken breast
4-oz. can sliced mushrooms, drained
¼ tsp. tarragon flakes
1 tsp. celery flakes
1 tbsp. parsley flakes
salt and pepper to taste
10-oz. can cream of mushroom soup
4 tbsps. sherry
¼ cup light cream
½ tsp. paprika

The How
Arrange the chicken breasts in casserole. Sprinkle with mushrooms and seasonings. Blend all the liquid ingredients well and pour over chicken. Cover and bake for 1½ hours at 325°. *Serves 4.*

Fish in Celery Sauce
Sherry works its magic in this quick and delightful gourmet dish.

The What
1 lb. filet of sole, sea bass, or other fish of your choice
1 can condensed cream of celery soup

¼ cup light cream
1 tsp. lemon juice
¼ cup sherry
2 tbsps. chopped parsley, or 1 tbsp. flakes
¼ cup grated Parmesan cheese

The How
Arrange filets in casserole. Mix all other ingredients well and pour over fish. Bake uncovered at 375° for 25 minutes in preheated oven.

Beef and Olive Casserole
The What
4 strips bacon, diced
1 large onion, chopped
2 lbs. stewing beef, cubed
flour
1 cup red wine, medium or dry
1 8-oz. can tomato sauce
1 bay leaf, broken in quarters
¼ tsp. thyme
¼ tsp. marjoram
1 cup pitted ripe olives, halved
2 tbsps. chopped parsley
1 tsp. instant onion flakes

The How
Fry bacon and onion together slowly until light brown. Dredge meat with flour, add to pan, and brown on all sides. Add balance of ingredients except olives and parsley. Transfer to casserole. Cover and bake at 300° for 2 hours until meat is tender. Add olives and parsley. Heat 5 minutes and serve with buttered noodles.

3. That Jiffy Electric Skillet

The electric skillet (or electric frying pan) is a versatile aid to the lady in a hurry. With a little attention to time and temperature, it can take a lot of the work out of meal preparation. With a little know-how and a little experience it's no trick to be a skillet chef. On those hot summer days you can prepare meals with oven-baked flavor without radiating the heat of an oven in your kitchen. The following 21 skillet dishes are hearty, tasty and satisfying.

Chicken Paprika
With that continental touch.

The What
6 drumsticks and thighs of chicken
¼ cup flour
5 tbsps. shortening
1 10½-oz. can condensed tomato soup
½ cup water
2 tbsps. instant minced onion
1 4-oz. can sliced mushrooms, drained
2 tsps. paprika

½ tsp. dried rosemary, or thyme
½ tsp. salt
¼ tsp. pepper
2 tsps. flour
½ cup dairy sour cream

The How
Coat chicken pieces well with flour. Brown evenly all over in the shortening. Mix tomato soup, water, seasonings, mushrooms, and onion. Pour on chicken, cover skillet, and cook at 325° until chicken is tender, about 30 to 35 minutes. Remove chicken to warm platter. Blend sour cream and 2 teaspoons flour together. Mix in some of the hot gravy, then return sour cream mixture to pan. Stir-cook until thickened. Return chicken to pan and hold hot until served. *Serves 4 to 6.*

Anchovy Potato Pudding
This is a Scandinavian delicacy that is best served with pickled beets and sliced cold sausage.

The What
5 large potatoes, sliced
1 can anchovy filets
2 eggs, beaten lightly
2 cups milk
1 tbsp. parsley flakes
2 tbsps. butter
2 tbsps. grated Parmesan cheese

The How
Melt butter in skillet. Arrange alternate layers of potatoes and anchovy filets. Top with parsley flakes and

Parmesan cheese. Mix eggs and milk and pour over potatoes. Cover and cook about 25 to 30 minutes until potatoes are tender. *Serves 4.*

One Dish Spaghetti
This is good indoors, or even cooked outdoors if you have the electrical outlet. Arrange all the ingredients on a tray, then amaze your guests with your culinary efforts.

The What
1 lb. minced beef
1 large onion, chopped
2 garlic cloves, minced
6-oz. can tomato paste
8-oz. can tomato sauce
1½ cups tomato juice
3 tbsps. celery flakes
3 tbsps. green pepper flakes
1½ cups water
¾ tsp. chili powder
1½ tsps. salt
1 tsp. sugar
1 tsp. oregano flakes
½ cup grated Parmesan cheese
8 ozs. uncooked spaghetti

The How
Put all ingredients except the last two in skillet. Stir to mix and break up meat well while bringing to a boil. Cover and simmer 30 minutes at 250°. Stir once or twice in that time. Break up spaghetti, add to pan, cover, and simmer another 20 minutes until spaghetti is just right. Sprinkle with cheese and serve to 6 happy people.

Swiss Scramble

This makes a fast, light, and tasty meal served with buttered toast and sliced tomatoes or tossed salad.

The What
6 eggs
¼ cup light cream or condensed milk
3 tbsps. soft butter
1 cup shredded Swiss cheese
4½-oz. can deviled ham
salt and pepper to taste
¼ tsp. paprika

The How
Beat the eggs lightly and stir in the cream, salt and pepper, and paprika. Melt the butter in the skillet, and pour in egg mixture. As it starts to bubble, stir in cheese and deviled ham. Stir-cook until set to your taste. *Serves 4.*

Goulash Vienna

This is a tender, delicate skillet stew that combines with sour cream and noodles for a delightful meal.

The What
2½ lbs. boneless veal or pork
4 tbsps. butter
4 onions, thinly sliced, or 2 tbsps. onion flakes
1 tbsp. paprika
1 cup dry white wine
1 can tomatoes
1 tbsp. chicken soup base
½ lb. mushrooms, sliced
1 cup dairy sour cream

1 tsp. oregano or marjoram flakes
3 cups buttered noodles

The How
Cut meat into cubes, dust with flour, and brown lightly in butter. Add onions and cook until soft. Add all ingredients except mushrooms, noodles, and sour cream and simmer covered at 225° for 2 hours. Stir in mushrooms, noodles, and sour cream. Reheat and serve to 6 or 8 lucky diners.

Skillet Braised Beef—Blackfriar's Roast
The slow simmering possible with the electric skillet makes a wonderful dish of the cheaper cuts of beef, such as chuck or brisket point, as in the following.

The What
2 lbs. chuck, 1½" thick
2 tbsps. salad oil
1 tbsp. lemon juice
1 bay leaf
6 peppercorns
1 tsp. salt
1 garlic clove, crushed
1 pint beef stock or consommé
2 tbsps. chopped parsley

The How
Brown beef on both sides in oil. Add balance of ingredients and simmer slowly at 250° until meat is tender.

Lamb Palermo
With the flavor of Italy.

That Jiffy Electric Skillet

The What
1 lb. boned lamb shoulder, cubed small
3 tbsps. flour
½ tsp. salt
¼ tsp. black pepper
½ tsp. chili powder
½ tsp. garlic powder or 1 crushed clove of garlic
2 medium potatoes, cubed
3 tbsps. oil or bacon dripping
¼ cup chopped parsley or 2 tbsps. flakes
1 cup boiling water
½ cup white wine
1 tbsp. minced onion flakes, or 3 tbsps. raw onion

The How
Mix flour, salt, and pepper in a paper bag. Shake lamb cubes until coated. Sauté lamb, garlic, and onion until meat is nicely browned. Add remaining ingredients and simmer covered about 1 hour at 225°. Add more wine or water if gravy becomes too thick. *Serves 3 or 4.*

Scampi Piquant
The What
2 5-oz. cans small shrimp, drained
4 tbsps. butter or margarine
¼ tsp. garlic powder or chips
2 tbsps. parsley flakes
½ cup white dinner wine, such as Chablis

The How
Melt butter in skillet. Add garlic, parsley, and wine and simmer 3 minutes. Add shrimp and heat. Serve with toast squares or rice as a meal, or from a chafing dish as an hors d'oeuvres.

Honey Chili
The kids love the taste of this one—fathers too.

The What
1 tbsp. oil
1 lb. ground beef
1 cup diced celery
2 tbsps. instant onion, or ½ cup chopped raw onion
1 can condensed tomato soup
½ tsp. salt
2 tsps. chili powder
2 tbsps. wine vinegar
¼ cup (4 tbsps.) honey
¼ tsp. oregano flakes

The How
Sauté beef in oil until red color is gone. Add onion and celery and stir-fry 3 minutes more. Add balance of ingredients and one cup water. Stir well. Cover and simmer at 225° for one hour, stirring occasionally.

Savory Ham and Rice
The What
3 cups instant rice, prepared as directed
2 tbsps. butter or margarine
½ lb. cooked ham, diced
2 tbsps. chopped parsley, or 1 tbsp. flakes
2 green onions, top and all, chopped
2 tbsps. honey, or 1 tbsp. brown sugar
1 tbsp. lemon juice
salt and pepper to taste

The How
Simmer onion in butter until soft. Add ham and stir-cook

3 minutes. Add balance of ingredients. Mix and heat. *Serves 4.*

Beef Noodle Stroganoff
The What
1 lb. ground beef
1 tsp. vegetable oil
1 can (16 ozs.) tomatoes
1 can (8 ozs.) tomato sauce
1½ tsps. salt
1½ tsps. sugar
¼ tsp. garlic powder
⅓ cup Burgundy
2 cups medium noodles
½ cup dairy sour cream

The How
Stir-cook meat in oil until red color is gone. Add next six ingredients and ½ cup water. Cover and simmer 10 minutes. Add noodles and simmer for an additional 20 minutes, covered. Add a little water if necessary. Stir in sour cream and serve. Also good without the sour cream, which can be served on the side to those who like it.

Spaghetti 'n Clam
The What
2 tbsps. olive oil
½ tsp. salt
½ tsp. garlic powder
1 tbsp. parsley flakes
¼ tsp. oregano or thyme
¼ tsp. black pepper
1 can (10 ozs.) minced clams

8 ozs. spaghetti, cooked and hot
1 tsp. cornstarch
grated Parmesan cheese

The How
Heat the first six ingredients in the oil. Mix cornstarch into the clam juice and stir-cook until thickened. Add clams and heat. Pour over spaghetti and sprinkle with Parmesan. A real yummy for lovers of clams—and spaghetti.

New England Sausage
The What
1 lb. brown-and-serve sausages
¼ cup butter or margarine
1 can pie sliced apples
nutmeg
flour

The How
Brown sausages in skillet. Remove. Add butter to skillet. Sprinkle apples with nutmeg and shake in flour until coated. Brown in butter and serve with sausage.

Glazed Ham Steak
The What
1 1½ lb. ready-to-eat ham slice, 1" thick
3 tbsps. orange marmalade
1 tsp. dry mustard
2 tbsps. butter or margarine

The How
Brown ham slice on both sides in butter. Mix marmalade

and mustard and spread on both sides of ham. Cook 2 minutes longer. *Serve to 4.*

Skillet Lasagna
The What
1 lb. ground beef
2 tbsps. butter or margarine
1 envelope spaghetti-sauce mix
1 lb. creamed cottage cheese
3 cups uncooked wide noodles
2 tsps. basil flakes
1 tbsp. parsley flakes
1 tsp. salt
¼ tsp. pepper
1 can (16 ozs.) tomatoes
1 can (8 ozs.) tomato sauce
½ lb. diced mozzarella cheese

The How
Fry meat in butter until gray in color. Sprinkle ½ spaghetti sauce mix, then spread on cottage cheese. Spread on noodles and seasonings. Pour tomatoes, tomato sauce, and 1 cup water over top. Bring to boil, and cover. Simmer 35 minutes. Sprinkle diced cheese on top and before serving let stand covered 5 minutes.

Hoe-Down Chowder
We are not sure if this makes the diner do a hoe-down or if the hoe-down makes him or her want the chowder. Anyway, the flavor is delightful.

The What
½ cup chopped onion
4 tbsps. butter

1 cup diced cooked ham or bacon
1 envelope cream of chicken soup mix
1½ cups fine-shredded cabbage
¼ tsp. dill flakes
½ cup sour cream
3 cups water

The How
Cook ham, cabbage, onion, and dill in butter, until onion is tender. Blend soup mix with water and add to pan. Add dill flakes and cabbage and simmer covered for 10 minutes. Add ham or bacon. Stir in sour cream and heat through. *Serves 4.*

Savory Veal Steak Parmigiana
The sauce with a zing complements the bland veal steak.

The What
1½ lbs. veal steak
2 tbsps. flour
¾ tsp. garlic powder
salt and pepper
3 tbsps. oil
¾ cup Rosé wine
⅓ cup dairy sour cream
⅓ cup grated Parmesan cheese
½ tsp. basil

The How
Cut steak into serving portions and dredge with flour, which has been mixed with the seasonings. Brown on both sides in oil. Drain off excess fat. Add wine, cover, and simmer 35 minutes at 250°. Mix Parmesan and sour

cream and spoon onto steak. Cover and cook 5 minutes longer. Serve with the sauce on the side to 4 favored guests.

Chili Vinos
The What
1 lb. ground beef
2 tbsps. oil or bacon fat
2 15-oz. cans chili con carne with beans
½ cup red dinner wine
4 hamburger buns
½ tsp. oregano flakes
1 tbsp. onion flakes
½ tsp. salt

The How
Shape beef into 4 patties the size of the buns. Brown well on both sides in fat. Pour wine, chili, and all other ingredients over meat and heat 5 minutes. To serve place a bun half in each plate, top with meat, then with other half of bun, and pour chili mixture over each bun.

Skillet Chicken Oahu
You can almost see the palm trees sway and the Hawaiian guitars moaning softly as you eat this Polynesian dish.

The What
2 lbs. chicken parts, small quarters or legs and wings
3 tbsps. butter or margarine
¼ tsp. pepper
1 envelope of cream of chicken soup mix
1 cup water
½ cup pineapple juice *from*

½ cup pineapple tidbits
1 dash cinnamon

The How
Heat pan to 375°. Brown chicken all over and sprinkle with pepper. Blend water, pineapple juice, and chicken soup mix. Add to chicken with cinnamon and pineapple. Cook covered at 250° for 25 minutes. Stir occasionally. *Serves 4 to 5.*

Savory Poached Eggs
A great start for a good day.

The What
1 tbsp. butter
1 tbsp. onion flakes
1 tbsp. flour
½ cup water
4 cloves
2 bay leaves
2 tbsps. vinegar (cider or malt)
¼ tsp. salt
1 tbsp. sugar
6 eggs

The How
Melt butter in skillet, add onion, and simmer until golden. Add flour and brown lightly. Add water, cloves, and bay leaves and stir-cook until smooth. Strain through a coarse sieve. Add vinegar, salt, and sugar and heat to boil. Break eggs into a wet saucer, one at a time, and slip into pan. Cover and cook until eggs are poached as you like them.

Potatoes Grillées
A beautifully crisp potato dish, full of golden beauty and taste.

The What
2 cans small potatoes
1 tbsp. parsley flakes, or 2 tbsps. fresh parsley
4 tbsps. butter
6 tbsps. bread crumbs

The How
Shake potatoes in butter at 350° until golden brown. Sprinkle on parsley and bread crumbs. Stir and shake until bread crumbs are crisp and golden. *Serves 4 to 6.*

4. Tricks with Instant Potatoes

Today is the "now" time for convenience potatoes. There are instant sliced, mashed, scalloped, and au gratin —all packaged and ready for the few touches that can make them into delightful dishes. Even the most tradition-minded French cooks now use them in preference to the older and more tedious methods of preparation. There are many easy and interesting ways to prepare and use the instant varieties beyond those listed on the package. Potatoes need never again be dull! The proof is in the following fast and easy dishes.

Five Minute Soup
Off the shelf and in a rush.

The What
1 10½-oz. can chicken or beef consommé
2 tbsps. butter
1 tbsp. flour
1 consommé can of hot water
¾ cup mashed potato flakes
½ tsp. salt

¼ tsp. savory
¼ tsp. pepper
3 tbsps. instant minced onion or flakes

The How
In a saucepan melt butter, add flour, and mix well. Add all other ingredients and stir-cook until slightly thickened. *Serves 4*

Sunny Eye Lunch
A light and quick dish.

The What
4 servings instant mashed potatoes
½ cup grated cheddar cheese
2 tbsps. butter
4 eggs
½ tsp. paprika (or parsley flakes)
salt and pepper

The How
Prepare potatoes as per package directions. Blend in the grated cheese. Spread in a shallow baking dish. Make four indentations in the potatoes with the bottom of a cup, large enough to hold one egg. Put ¼ of the butter in each indentation and break an egg into each. Brown 10 minutes in a 500° oven, or heat under broiler until eggs are done. Sprinkle with parsley or paprika. *Serves 4.*

Savory Kernels
Meat in a blanket.

The What
mashed potato

cocktail sausage or salmon
fine bread crumbs

The How
Prepare a thick mix of mashed potato. Take a large spoonful and form into a small cup. Put in a cocktail sausage or a spoon of salmon and mould potato into a ball with the meat in the center. Roll in crumbs and refrigerate 2 hours or more. Fry quickly in butter. A delightful lunch with a green or jellied salad.

Jiffy Casserole
The What
2½ cups instant sliced potatoes
1 can condensed cream of mushroom soup
1 cup of any leftover meats
1 10-oz. can tomato juice
1¼ cups boiling water
2 tbsps. onion flakes or diced onion
2 tbsps. green pepper flakes
¾ cup grated cheddar cheese
¼ tsp. black pepper
½ tsp. salt
2 tbsps. butter

The How
Mix butter, boiling water, and mushroom soup in casserole. Stir until blended. Add balance of ingredients, except cheese, and mix. Sprinkle with cheese. Bake uncovered at 375° for 45 minutes.

Potatoes Western
The What
6 slices bacon

Tricks with Instant Potatoes

2 cups instant sliced potatoes
2 tbsps. onion flakes or diced onion
1 20-oz. can tomatoes
1 tsp. salt
¼ tsp. pepper
½ tsp. prepared mustard
1 tsp. sugar
½ tsp. celery powder

The How
Pan-fry bacon and drain on paper towel. Crumble. Prepare potatoes as directed on package. Drain well. Sauté in bacon drippings for 5 minutes with onion flakes. Add remaining ingredients and simmer 20 minutes. Sprinkle bacon on top and serve to 4.

Fast Stroganoff
The What
1 lb. hamburger
1 4-oz. can mushrooms
1 package au gratin potatoes
½ tsp. thyme
½ pint sour cream
¼ cup boiling water
salt and pepper

The How
While browning hamburger and mushrooms together, prepare potatoes as directed on package. Add boiling water, sauce mix, and sour cream. Add seasonings to meat and then combine everything together. Reheat. Serves 4.

Crunchy Au Gratin
The What
1 can cream of celery soup
1 tbsp. butter
1 package au gratin potatoes
2½ cups boiling water
4 slices cooked bacon, crumbled

The How
Spread potatoes in casserole. Add hot water and other ingredients and mix well. Bake uncovered at 375° for 45 minutes.

Instant Potato Salad
The What
3 hard-boiled eggs, chopped
1 tbsp. green pepper flakes
½ cup chopped celery
1 tbsp. onion flakes
½ tsp. salt
4 tbsps. mayonnaise
1 tbsp. vinegar
1 envelope (4 servings) instant potato flakes

The How
Add onion flakes, pepper flakes, and seasonings to potato flakes. Prepare as directed on package. Add hard boiled eggs, celery, mayonnaise, and vinegar and mix well. Chill and serve on lettuce. *Serves 4.*

Spud 'n Cheese Balls
The What
1¾ cups mashed potato flakes

1⅓ cups boiling water
⅓ cup cold milk
pinch of cayenne pepper
1 egg, beaten
½ cup fine bread or cracker crumbs
cubes of cheddar cheese, ¾ inch

The How
Prepare potatoes as directed on package, adding the pinch of cayenne. Form into balls over the cheese cubes—about the size of a golf ball. Roll in egg, then in crumbs. Bake in greased pan at 450° for 15 minutes. *Serves 4.*

Potato Florentine
For spinach lovers.

The What
1¾ cups instant mashed potato
1 cup cooked spinach, drained
2 tbsps. butter
1⅓ cups boiling water
½ cup cold milk
2 cups bread cubes, browned in butter

The How
Mix the potato flakes with boiling water. Add butter and milk and mix well. Mix in spinach. Top with bread croutons and heat 15 minutes in 450° oven.

Tuna Puffs
The What
1¾ cups instant potato
2 cups boiling water

3 tbsps. butter
2 cups flaked tuna, or other fish
1 tbsp. lemon juice
½ cup milk
1 tsp. Worcestershire sauce
1 tbsp. celery flakes
1 tbsp. parsley flakes
1 tbsp. green pepper flakes
1 tbsp. instant onion
3 eggs, separated

The How
Put all vegetable flakes in the boiling water. Add potato, lemon juice, butter, and fish. Add beaten egg yolks and beat mixture until light. Fold in stiffly beaten egg whites and pile lightly in greased casserole. Bake uncovered in 350° oven about 45 minutes until set and lightly browned. *Serves 6 to 8.*

Cheeseburger Pie
The What
1 lb. ground beef
2 tbsps. onion flakes
2 tbsps. celery flakes (or ½ cup chopped celery)
½ tsp. oregano
1 tsp. salt
¼ tsp. pepper
½ cup cracker crumbs
½ cup tomato sauce
1 cup grated cheddar cheese
1¾ cups potato flakes

The How
Sauté meat and vegetable flakes until meat is browned.

Tricks with Instant Potatoes

Add seasonings, cracker crumbs, and tomato sauce and mix well. Prepare potatoes as directed on package. Line a large pie pan or shallow casserole with the potatoes. Spoon in meat mixture. Top with the cheese. Bake in preheated 350° oven 30 minutes. Brown under broiler. *Serves 6.*

Lazy Shepherd's Pie
The What
2 cups ground or chopped leftover meat
1 cup gravy (canned is o.k.)
2 tbsps. instant minced onion
¾ cup sliced or diced cooked carrot
¾ cup cooked peas
½ tsp. salt
¼ tsp. pepper
1 tsp. Worcestershire sauce
½ tsp. oregano
1 small can kernel corn
1¾ cups mashed potato flakes
½ cup grated cheese

The How
Heat the gravy. Put half of it in casserole and mix in all ingredients except the cheese and potato. Prepare the potatoes as directed on package, using remainder of gravy as part of required liquid. Spoon onto top of mixture in casserole. Top with cheese. Bake 20 minutes at 350°; then heat under broiler until cheese melts and potatoes are golden. *Serves 4 or 5.*

Ceylon Chicken Pie
It's snappy, tasty, and best of all quick!

The What
1 can condensed cream of chicken soup
2 cups diced cooked chicken
½ cup canned mushrooms
1 tsp. curry powder
1 tbsp. sherry
¼ tsp. salt
⅛ tsp. black pepper
3 tbsps. grated cheddar cheese
¼ tsp. paprika
1¾ cups mashed potato flakes
½ cup pineapple juice

The How
Preheat oven to 425°. Prepare potato as directed on package, using pineapple juice instead of milk. Line a large pie plate with the potatoes, and allow to set, while mixing all other ingredients except cheese. Put filling in potato crust, sprinkle on cheese, and bake at 425° until crust is golden. *Serves 4 to 6.*

Down Country Chowder
Good country fare—and good anywhere else, too.

The What
6 slices side bacon
2 tbsps. instant onion
2 tbsps. celery flakes
1½ cups boiling water
3 cups milk
½ tsp. thyme
1 tsp. salt

¼ tsp. pepper
1¾ cups instant potato flakes

The How
Fry bacon until crisp and crumble back into pan, leaving 2 tablespoons fat. Add boiling water, vegetable flakes, and seasonings. Add milk and bring to simmer. Stir in potato flakes until chowder is thickened. *Serves 4 to 6.*

Stuffed Peppers
Sudden style.

The What
6 large green peppers
6 wieners, sliced thin *or*
6 cooked sausage, sliced
1 tbsp. butter
2½ cups boiling water
⅓ cup fine bread crumbs
1 package au gratin instant potato
¼ tsp. sage
1 tbsp. instant onion
½ tsp. salt
¼ tsp. pepper

The How
Cut tops off peppers, remove seeds, blanch 3 minutes in boiling water, and drain well. Combine potato slices, au gratin sauce mix, butter, sausage slices, and boiling water in saucepan with seasonings. Simmer 20 minutes. Stuff peppers with mixture. Top with crumbs and bake 20 minutes at 350°. *Serves 6.*

5. Quick Stunts with Sausage

Sausage has been an important meat staple for about 5000 years, and almost every country produces its own brands. The variety of fresh, cured, and smoked sausages is almost endless. Cooked sausages—such as frankfurters and bologna, Vienna, garlic, liverwurst, blutwurst, berliner, knablauch—are all readily available to suit almost every taste. The harder varieties—such as salami, pepperoni, cappicolo, and summer sausage—are used both in cooking and sandwich making. Fresh sausage—such as pork, beef, and a mixture of the two—are available in various sizes, shapes, and flavors.

Baked Sausage with Potato Stuffing
This is a hardy dish, much favored by men who work hard and eat well.

The What
4 slices bacon, diced
1 dozen pork sausage links
1 tbsp. onion flakes
2 cups mashed potatoes

1 tbsp. bacon dripping
4 cups stale bread, cubed
1 tsp. parsley flakes
¼ tsp. sage
½ tsp. marjoram
2 eggs, lightly beaten

The How
Fry sausages with a little water to extract fat. Pour off fat and set sausages aside. Sauté bacon and onion until brown. Add to potatoes with bacon dripping, bread cubes, parsley, and seasoning. Stir in beaten eggs. Put in baking pan and top with sausage. Bake at 375° for 30 to 40 minutes. *Serve with cole slaw to 6.*

Sausage Hawaiian
This one brings them off their lanais on the run to the table.

The What
1½ lbs. large pork farmer's style sausage
1 can (10 ozs.) mushrooms
15-oz. can pineapple chunks
2 tbsps. green pepper flakes
1 tbsp. onion flakes
1½ tbsps. cornstarch
mushroom and pineapple liquid with water to make 2 cups
⅓ cup molasses
¼ cup vinegar

The How
Brown the sausage and pour off the fat. Add all but ½

cup of the liquid and simmer 15 minutes. Mix vinegar and molasses and add with mushrooms, green pepper, and onion. Simmer 10 minutes. Dissolve cornstarch in remaining ½ cup of liquid and add to pan. Cook until slightly thickened. Add pineapple chunks. Heat and serve over hot rice.

Heaven Hash
This is quick and very tasty indeed.

The What
1 lb. sausage meat, fried and chopped
3 cups mashed potato (instant if you wish)
½ cup stock or gravy (bouillon cube is o.k.), or canned gravy if you have it
1 envelope onion soup mix
¼ tsp. savory
3 tbsps. red wine (optional)
¼ cup sliced mushrooms (for the gourmet)

The How
Mix all ingredients except wine and season with salt and pepper to taste. Use just enough stock or gravy to moisten ingredients so they can be spread in the skillet. Cover and let steam through (5 minutes). Cook 10 minutes until crusted on bottom. Turn and cook 6 minutes more. *Note:* Any leftover meat can be used for this hash. For a change in taste, mix the instant mashed potato with hot tomato juice. Use ½ teaspoon curry powder instead of the savory.

Sausage and Lima Casserole
The What
2 pkgs. frozen Lima beans

Quick Stunts with Sausage

1 lb. pork sausage links
¼ tsp. garlic powder
2 tbsps. onion flakes
1 tbsp. green pepper flakes
1 can condensed tomato soup
1 tbsp. celery flakes
1 tbsp. sugar
¼ tsp. pepper
½ tsp. salt
½ tsp. dry mustard
⅓ cup dry white wine
½ cup grated sharp cheese

The How
Fry sausage until browned. Cook Limas in 1 cup boiling water with the celery, onion, and pepper flakes and the seasonings. Add the wine and put bean mixture in casserole. Top with sausage in wheel spoke design. Cover and bake ½ hour at 350°. Remove cover, top with cheese, and bake 20 minutes.

Sausage and Sweet Potato Casserole
The What
1 lb. (2 pkgs.) brown-and-serve sausages
1 cup applesauce
1 tbsp. lemon juice
2 cups mashed sweet potato
1 tbsp. melted butter
½ tsp. salt
¼ tsp. ground cloves
¼ tsp. cinnamon
2 eggs, beaten
sprinkle of nutmeg
1 tsp. onion flakes

The How
Brown sausage lightly. Mix all other ingredients well and put in casserole. Top with sausage links. Cover and bake 30 minutes at 375°. Uncover and bake 10 minutes. *Note:* Try mashed squash instead of sweet potato for a variation in taste.

Sausage-Stuffed Eggplant
The What
1 large or 2 medium eggplants
1 lb. bulk pork sausage meat
2 tbsps. onion flakes or 1 large onion, chopped
½ tsp. garlic powder
2 tbsps. celery flakes
2 tbsps. green pepper flakes
1 16-oz. can tomatoes
½ tsp. basil
1 tsp. salt
¼ tsp. pepper
½ tsp. sugar
¼ cup dry bread crumbs
¼ cup Parmesan cheese

The How
Cut eggplant in half lengthwise and parboil 10 minutes in salted water. Mash sausage thin and brown quickly on both sides. Remove and drain on paper towel. Chop fine. When eggplant is cool, scoop out all the pulp to leave about ½" shell. Chop eggplant pulp and add to pan with 2 tablespoons fat, tomatoes, and balance of ingredients except cheese and bread crumbs. Add sausage and simmer 10 minutes. Put in greased baking dish. Top with crumbs mixed with cheese. Bake 40 minutes at 375°. *Serves 4 to 6.*

Quick Stunts with Sausage

Sausage Hot Pot
The What
1 lb. brown-and-serve sausage
2 tbsps. instant minced onion
4 large potatoes, sliced thin
1 pkg. frozen French-style green beans
1 cup sliced mushrooms
2 tbsps. butter
2 tbsps. flour
1 cup stock or bouillon
1 tsp. salt
1 tsp. dry mustard
½ tsp. Worcestershire sauce
½ cup evaporated milk

The How
Brown sausage lightly and set aside. Put half of it in bottom of greased casserole. Layer on half of potatoes and sprinkle with half the onion. Add all of the beans (thawed). Add remainder of sausage, then remaining potatoes. Add 2 tablespoons butter to pan and stir in flour until smooth. Add stock and seasonings and stir-cook until thickened. Add mushrooms and pour into casserole. Bake covered at 350° for 1½ hours. Uncover and brown for 20 minutes. *Serves 4 to 6.*

Sausage in Ale (English Style)
The What
1 lb. link pork sausage
1 cup ale
2 bay leaves
5 or 6 peppercorns
5 whole cloves

buttered toast
chopped parsley

The How
Put sausage in cold skillet. Cook slowly over low heat until lightly browned all over. Pour off fat and add ale and spices tied in a bag. Simmer covered for ½ hour. Add more ale if needed. Serve on toast with scrambled eggs to 4 or 5. *A switch.* Use cocktail sausages simmered in red wine with a spice bag, but no bay leaf.

Sausage Toss Pot
In England a toss pot is a drunk, but don't confuse the issue by thinking.

The What
1 lb. fresh pork sausage links, cut 1 inch long
1 small head of cabbage, shredded
1 tsp. salt
¼ tsp. pepper
2 tbsps. dry wine
1 tsp. caraway seed (optional) or savory
1 pkg. (8 ozs.) fine noodles

The How
Brown sausage chunks and pour off all but 2 tablespoons fat. Braise cabbage, stirring often, until just tender. Cook noodles according to package directions. Add to pan with sausage and toss together with seasonings and wine. Cook covered 10 minutes. *Serves 6 or more, depending on appetites.*

Crown Jewel Pie
It doesn't sparkle. The term is related to its gourmet taste!

Quick Stunts with Sausage

The What
pastry for 2-crust pie
1 lb. brown-and-serve sausage links
4 leeks, or 8 green onions, chopped
2 tbsps. butter
2 tbsps. flour
salt and pepper to taste
½ cup condensed milk
1 tbsp. horseradish
½ cup chopped pistachio nuts
½ cup apple, diced
pinch of nutmeg
1 cup stock or bouillon

The How
Cut sausage in ½ inch slices and brown in butter. Remove. Sauté leeks or onions and apple until tender. Remove. Add flour to pan, and cook-stir until smooth. Add stock, milk, and seasonings and cook until thick. Add apple, leeks or onions, horseradish, and nuts. Pour into pie shell, over sausage, and sprinkle with nutmeg. Put on top crust and prick to let out steam. Bake at 425° for ½ hour, or until crust is golden. *Serves 6 very well indeed.*

Wiener Roast with Sauerkraut
The What
16 wieners
1 can (28 ozs.) sauerkraut
2 tbsps. onion flakes
½ cup apple, chopped
4 strips bacon
¼ cup grated cheddar cheese

½ cup bread crumbs, soft
¼ cup apple juice

The How
Wash the sauerkraut and drain. Put in saucepan with apple juice. Add the apple and sprinkle on the onion flakes. Cover and steam for 10 minutes. Put in greased casserole. Layer on the wieners and then the bacon strips. Mix cheese and crumbs and spread on top. Bake uncovered at 375° for 30 minutes. *Serves 5 or 6.*

Scalloped Sausage and Corn
The What
1½ lbs. pork sausage meat
2 cups cream-style corn
8 soda crackers, crumbled
1 egg, beaten
1 cup milk
½ tsp. salt
1 good pinch of each: pepper, cayenne, nutmeg
1 large tomato, sliced thin
1 tbsp. onion flakes

The How
Make small balls of half the sausage. Brown the balls and balance of sausage. Drain on paper towels. Crumble the sausage that was not made into balls. Mix crumbled sausage with corn, crackers, milk, egg, onion flakes, and seasonings. Pour into greased casserole. Layer on the tomato slices and top them with the sausage balls. Place casserole in 1 inch of water in a pan. Cover and bake at 350° for 45 minutes. Uncover and bake 15 minutes, or until firmly set. *Serves 6.*

Quick Stunts with Sausage

Polish Bigos
The What
2 cups diced cooked meat (left over)
1 lb. kielbassa sausage
1 can (28 ozs.) sauerkraut
1 can (16 ozs.) tomatoes
1 large onion, chopped
1 large apple, chopped
1 tbsp. bacon fat
¼ tsp. pepper
½ tsp. salt
½ tsp. dry mustard
1 tbsp. sugar
1 tbsp. flour
1 can mushrooms, stems and pieces, drained
2 cups meat stock

The How
Drain and rinse sauerkraut. Put in heavy pot with stock and liquid from tomatoes, and bring to simmer. Sauté tomatoes, apple, and onion in fat for 5 minutes, stirring. Cut kielbassa in one inch chunks and add to pan. Simmer 10 minutes. Add seasonings, sugar, cooked meat, and flour to pan and stir-cook until slightly thickened. Add mushrooms. Add contents of pan to pot, and simmer for 1½ hours. This dish is better if eaten the day after it was cooked. It also freezes well. Serve with boiled potatoes to 6 or 8 who like traditional Polish cooking.

Quick Sausage Casserole
The What
1 lb. fresh pork sausage
1 can (20 ozs.) sliced apples

2 tbsps. flour
2 tbsps. lemon juice
¼ tsp. salt
pinch of clove, cinnamon, nutmeg
1 cup grated sharp cheddar cheese

The How
Brown sausage and pour off all but 2 tablespoons fat. Put sausage in greased casserole. Drain apple slices and reserve juice. Put apple slices on top of sausage. Put flour in fat in pan and stir smooth. Stir in apple juice, lemon juice, and seasonings. Pour over apples and sausage. Sprinkle on cheese. Bake uncovered at 350° for 45 minutes.

Sausage and Red Beans
The What
1 lb. pork sausage meat
2 tbsps. instant onion flakes
½ tsp. oregano
1 can (16 ozs.) red kidney beans
1 can cream of celery soup
½ soup can water

The How
Shape sausage into 10 or 12 patties and pan brown. Pour off fat and add balance of ingredients. Heat and serve.

Sausage-Stuffed Acorn Squash
The What
1 lb. pork sausage meat
2 acorn squash
2 tbsps. onion flakes
1½ cups soft bread crumbs

1 tsp. salt
¼ tsp. pepper
½ tsp. thyme

The How
Cut squash in half and remove seeds. Put 1 inch water in skillet. Place squash in—cut side down—and steam for 10 minutes. Mash sausage and brown in pan. Drain fat. Mix meat, onion flakes, seasonings, and bread crumbs. Mound in squash. Bake at 375° for 30 minutes. *Serves 4.*

6. Blender Specialties

Owning a blender is like having an extra pair of hands, or an unsalaried kitchen helper. A little time spent in learning the capabilities of this tremendously versatile appliance is your membership in applied wizardry. When you are on familiar terms with your blender, you will wonder how you ever prepared meals without it.

The secret of blender cookery is learning what a blender will and will not do. First, remember that no blender will knead stiff dough, beat egg whites for frosting, grind raw meat (it purees it), or whip cream (it turns to butter right in front of your eyes). However, you'll be surprised at the versatile jobs your blender will do. You can shred or chop small quantities of raw turnip, carrots, celery, or other fibrous vegetables, provided you dice them first. Use a rubber or wooden spatula to push vegetables down from sides of container—and be careful. A blender will also shred your spatula, or a finger! You can shred cooked meats for soups, and also parsley, watercress, shallots, and leeks. If you are shredding meats, some will stick to the sides of the container and will not feed to the blades. A small amount of dry bread added with the meat will prevent this.

The blender is wonderful for making crumbs. You can use bread, graham crackers, zwiebach, dry toast, pretzels, or any dry cereal to make crumbs for any purpose. You can grate hard cheeses such as Parmesan if you cube the cheese first. Oily cheese may be grated with a little dry bread. Hard cereal grains such as beans or lentils can be cracked to cut down cooking time in soups. Rice or bean flour can be made from whole grains.

The following recipes direct you step by step in using your blender to cut the time of preparation for a variety of delicious kitchen-tested foods.

APPETIZERS

Cheese Dip
Many delicious dips start with basic cheese dip, so here's a good one.

The What
1/3 cup chicken stock (or milk)
2 ozs. strong cheddar cheese
6 ozs. cream cheese
2 ozs. blue cheese
6 ozs. cottage cheese
1/8 tsp. garlic powder
1/4 tsp. celery salt
dash of Tabasco sauce

The How
Blend for 20 seconds on high speed. This makes a pint

of smooth, zingy dip. Excellent with potato sticks, vegetable sticks, or crackers.

Blue Cheese Dip
The What

1 cup creamy cottage cheese
¼ medium onion
6 stalks watercress
⅓ cup cream
1 tsp. Worcestershire sauce
4 ozs. blue cheese

The How

Cover and blend until smooth and creamy. Delicious dip for hot french fries—or cold potato chips. Unique as a pretzel dip.

Beer Cheese Dip
The What

8 ozs. cheddar cheese, cubed
8 ozs. cream cheese
¾ cup beer
¼ tsp. garlic powder
⅓ cup diced dill pickle

The How

Blend cream cheese with ½ cup beer on high speed for 7 seconds. Add garlic powder, balance of beer, and dill pickle. Blend for 10 seconds. Add cheddar cheese and blend 10 seconds longer.

Clam Dip
The What

6 ozs. cream cheese

1 can (7½ ozs.) minced clams
¼ tsp. celery salt
1 tbsp. chopped green onion top (or chive flakes)
1 tsp. chervil flakes
dash of Tabasco

The How
Drain clams and reserve ¼ cup of juice. Add the juice and half the clams to blender container, with cream cheese, onion, and seasonings. Blend 10 seconds. Add balance of clams and blend 2 seconds. Chill before serving.

Chicken Liver Dip
The What
½ lb. chicken livers, cut coarsely
1 hard-boiled egg, cut in eighths
¼ tsp. celery pepper
¼ tsp. thyme
½ tsp. salt
2 slices bacon, diced
2 tbsps. butter
2 tbsps. chicken fat
1 medium onion, diced

The How
Sauté bacon, chicken livers, and onion in butter and chicken fat for 8 minutes. Put it all in the blender. Add balance of ingredients and blend 5 seconds on high speed. Make sure all ingredients have been well blended. Scrape out and chill.

Guacamole Dip
The What
1 ripe avocado, peeled and sliced

3 tbsps. lemon juice
4 tbsps. olive oil
1 clove garlic
¼ tsp. cayenne pepper
¼ tsp. salt

The How
Blend all together on high speed, stopping once to stir down. Usually served with sesame seed crackers or small sesame seed finger rolls.

Instant Onion Dip
The What
1 pint sour cream
1 tsp. lemon juice
1 package onion soup mix

The How
Blend ingredients on high speed for 10 seconds. Let chill for 2 hours to develop full flavor before serving.

Ham Dip
You may also use chicken.

The What
¾ cup diced cooked ham
½ small onion
⅛ tsp. cloves
⅛ tsp. nutmeg
1 tsp. Worcestershire sauce
dash of Tabasco
½ cup mayonnaise

Blender Specialties

The How
Blend thoroughly about 20 seconds. Let sit for 2 hours to develop flavor.

Hickory Cheese Dip
The What
6 ozs. cream cheese
6 ozs. diced hickory smoked cheese
⅓ cup pineapple juice
¼ tsp. Worcestershire sauce
1 tsp. tomato paste or sauce
1 clove garlic, or ¼ tsp. garlic powder
¼ tsp. salt

The How
Blend cream cheese and pineapple juice. Add balance of ingredients and blend 25 seconds. Chill before serving.

Barbecue Dip
The What
1 cup creamy cottage cheese
¼ cup soft butter
½ cup chili sauce
1 tbsp. prepared horseradish
1 tbsp. lemon juice

The How
Blend for 20 seconds and cool before serving.

NOTE
These dips are only a few of the dozens of flavor combinations possible with a blender. You can let your

imagination rove to its limits of gourmet concept in the invention of new and delicious combinations. The individual touch will be appreciated.

BLENDER BEVERAGES

Coffee Tropical
Fill blender container one half full of crushed ice. Add 1 tablespoon sugar and 1 cup strong black coffee. Blend on high speed until frothy and smooth.

Orange Apricot Nectar
Put in container:
2 cups orange juice
3 tbsps. lemon juice
1 cup cracked ice
½ cup cooked apricots

Cover and blend on high speed 10 seconds.

Mocha Float
Put in container:
1½ squares unsweetened chocolate pieces. Add ¼ cup boiling water. Blend on high speed 5 seconds. Add 2 teaspoons instant coffee, 3 tablespoons sugar, pinch of salt, and 1½ cups cold milk. Blend on high speed for 15 seconds. Pour in glasses and top with vanilla ice cream.

Pineapple-Banana Cream
Put in container:
½ cup dry milk powder
1½ cups pineapple juice
1 sliced banana

Blend 15 seconds, then add 2 scoops vanilla ice cream. Blend 15 seconds and serve in tall glasses.

Grasshopper
Blend for 10 seconds on low speed:
2 ozs. green creme de menthe
2 ozs. creme de cacao
2 ozs. heavy cream
½ cup crushed ice

Strain into cocktail glasses.

Alexander
A Grasshopper with brandy in place of creme de menthe.

Screwdriver
Put in container:
4 ozs. vodka
½ cup crushed ice
1½ cups orange juice

Blend 15 seconds on low speed, 5 seconds on high. Strain into highball glasses.

Whiskey Sour
Put in container:
1 cup crushed ice
2 ozs. lemon juice
8 ozs. rye or bourbon
1 oz. sugar syrup

Cover and blend for 5 seconds.

Stinger
Put in container:
3 ozs. brandy
½ cup crushed ice
3 ozs. white creme de menthe
Blend 10 seconds on high speed. Strain into cocktail glasses.

Darwin Daiquiri
Put in container:
1 oz. lime juice
2 ozs. orange juice
2 tsps. sugar
3 ozs. white rum
1 cup crushed ice
1 dash Angostura bitters

Blend on high speed for 10 seconds. *Serves 2.*

Basic Daiquiri
Put in container:
3 ozs. white rum
1½ tbsps. lime juice
1 tbsp. sugar
1 cup crushed ice

Blend 10 seconds on high speed.

Fruit Daiquiri
Put in container:
3 ozs. light rum
2 tbsps. lime juice
1 tbsp. sugar

¼ cup fruit cocktail
1 cup crushed ice

Blend on high speed 10 seconds. *Serves 2.*

Hawaiian Blossom
Put in container:
4 ozs. light rum
8 ozs. pineapple juice
½ oz. lime juice
½ oz. lemon juice
1 tbsp. sugar
1 cup crushed ice
1 tbsp. Maraschino cherry juice

Cover and blend on low speed 20 seconds. Strain into cocktail glasses.

PANCAKES AND WAFFLES

Basic Pancakes
The What
1 cup milk
1 cup pancake mix
1 tbsp. cooking oil
1 egg
½ tsp. sugar

The How
Put milk into container. Add egg and oil. Blend 3 seconds. Add flour and blend until flour is well mixed, about 5 seconds.

Chocolate Waffles
The What
3 tsps. double-acting baking powder
2 cups sifted all-purpose flour
2 ozs. unsweetened chocolate, cut up
½ cup hot milk
½ cup sugar
3 eggs
½ tsp. salt
¼ cup melted butter
½ tsp. vanilla
1 cup milk

The How
Sift flour and baking powder into mixing bowl. Put chocolate and hot milk into blender and blend 20 seconds on high speed. Add eggs, sugar, salt, butter, and vanilla. Blend 5 seconds. Add the cup of milk and blend 10 seconds. Pour over dry ingredients and mix lightly. Bake as you would any other waffle mix.

Orange Pancakes
The What
1 egg
1 cup orange juice
3 tbsps. cooking oil
¼ cup milk
½ tsp. salt
2½ tsps. double-acting baking powder
1½ cups sifted all-purpose flour
3 tbsps. sugar

The How
Put liquids in blender first. Blend on low speed until

egg is well blended, 5 seconds. Add dry ingredients and blend on high speed 10 seconds. Serve with orange sauce (see sauces).

Foolproof Popovers
The What
1 cup flour
¼ tsp. salt
1 tsp. sugar
⅞ cup milk
2 eggs
1 tbsp. melted butter

The How
Blend all ingredients until smooth. Preheat oven to 450°. Butter popover pans and heat until hissing hot. Pour ⅓ full. Bake 20 minutes at 450°, then lower heat to 350° and bake 15 minutes longer. Makes 8 popovers.

Green Corn Pancake
The What
2 cups green corn, cut off cob, *or*
2 cups tender corn niblets
¼ cup milk
1 egg and 1 egg yolk extra (save white)
1 tsp. sugar
½ tsp. salt
1½ tbsps. soft butter
½ tsp. grated nutmeg
½ tsp. freshly ground pepper

The How
Blend all ingredients together on high, except egg, for 10 seconds. Add egg and blend on low for 5 seconds. Sift

1 cup all-purpose flour with 1 teaspoon baking powder. Stir in puree from blender. Beat egg white and fold in. Use a thin bacon gravy with 2 tablespoons pancake syrup added. *For a real taste sensation* use oyster liquor instead of milk and drop 3 or 4 small oysters into the batter right after you put it on the griddle. Do not overcook. Serve with crisp bacon curls and pepper relish or coleslaw.

Blueberry Pancakes
The What

½ cup coarsely crushed cornflakes (put cornflakes in blender on low and run until just crushed. Pour into bowl.)
2 cups cake flour, *sifted with*
¼ cup fine sugar
1 tsp. salt
3 eggs
¼ cup cooking oil
1¼ cups milk
1 11-oz. pkg. frozen blueberries, separated but not thawed

The How

Blend together eggs, oil, and milk for 5 seconds. Pour into dry mixture and stir well. Add blueberries and stir lightly. Serve with cream cheese sauce. *Serves 4 to 6.*

Cream Cheese Sauce
The What

3 ozs. orange juice
½ tsp. grated rind of orange
¼ cup liquid honey
8-oz. pkg. cream cheese

The How
Peel off thin slices of orange rind and put in blender with orange juice. Blend on high speed 20 seconds. Add honey with blender on low speed. Drop in chunks of cream cheese and blend until smooth.

BLENDER HOT ENTREES

Beef Rolls
The What
2 tbsps. oil
4 thin slices top round beef
¼ lb. pork sausage meat
¼ small onion
½ cup parsley clusters
1 egg
⅛ tsp. black pepper
½ tsp. salt
1 can (4 ozs.) mushrooms
1 tomato, quartered
¾ small onion
½ tsp. salt
½ tsp. oregano
¼ tsp. thyme
1 stalk celery, cut up
2 tbsps. flour
¼ cup red wine

The How
Blend on high speed for 30 seconds: drained mushrooms (reserve liquid), ¼ onion, egg, pepper, ½ teaspoon salt, and parsley clusters. Spread on rounds of beef, roll up,

and tie. Brown in oil on all sides. Blend wine, mushroom liquid, tomato, ¾ onion, celery, and seasonings 10 seconds on high speed. Add to beef rolls, cover, and simmer slowly 1 hour. Remove string from rolls and serve with sauce.

Meat Loaf
The What
2 lbs. ground round of beef
½ lb. ground lean pork
2 slices bread
2 eggs
¾ cup tomato sauce
1 stalk celery, cut up, leaves and all
1 tsp. oregano
2 tsps. salt
½ tsp. black pepper
½ tsp. M.S.G.
¼ tsp. garlic powder
1 tbsp. Worcestershire sauce
1 tbsp. lemon juice

The How
Blender crumb the bread. Mix well with beef and pork. Put tomato sauce and eggs in blender. Blend 5 seconds on low speed. Add balance of ingredients and blend 30 seconds on high speed. Mix thoroughly with meat. Bake in loaf pan at 350° for 1½ hours. Tangy and flavorful.

Cheese Noodles
The What
8-oz. pkg. noodles, cooked
1½ cups hot milk

¼ tsp. thyme
1 tsp. salt
¼ cup soft butter
⅛ tsp. white pepper
2 tbsps. chive flakes
2 cups cubed cheddar
1 oz. blue cheese
¼ cup flour

The How
Blend all ingredients except noodles and flour 15 seconds on high speed. Switch to low and add flour. Put noodles in buttered baking dish and pour on sauce. Bake in 350° oven for 30 minutes.

Zippy Cheese Casserole

The What
8 ozs. elbow macaroni, cooked
½ lb. pork sausage meat, fried and drained
4 egg yolks
4 egg whites
½ small onion
1½ cups nippy cheese, cubed
½ cup melted butter
1 tsp. salt
½ tsp. black pepper
¼ tsp. savory
¼ tsp. M.S.G.

The How
Blend all ingredients, except macaroni, pork, and egg whites, on high speed for 20 seconds. Add pork and

blend 5 seconds more. Put in mixing bowl with macaroni and mix well. Beat egg whites until stiff and fold in. Bake in buttered casserole or baking dish 30 to 35 minutes in preheated 350° oven.

Creole Linguini

The What

1 pkg. (8 ozs.) linguini
2 slices bread
¼ cup powdered Parmesan or Romano Cheese
1 pkg. frozen spinach
1 tbsp. instant onion
¼ tsp. garlic powder
½ tsp. salt
½ tsp. oregano flakes
½ cup chicken stock, or bouillon
½ tsp. chili powder
2 tbsps. tomato sauce
1 tbsp. lemon juice
¾ cup coffee cream

The How

Cook linguini as directed on package. Drain and rinse. Crumb bread in blender. Remove and mix with cheese. Cook spinach in chicken stock, covered, for 10 minutes after starting to boil. Put stock and spinach in blender and add balance of ingredients, except bread, cheese, and linguini. Blend 20 seconds on high speed. Put layers of linguini and layers of sauce in casserole. Top with cheese crumb mixture. Bake uncovered 30 minutes at 350°.

Spinach Timbales
The What
1 hard-boiled egg

3 slices bread
3½ cups cooked, drained spinach
¼ cup cream
3 eggs
½ tsp. salt
2 tbsps. melted butter
½ tsp. oregano flakes
½ tsp. thyme flakes
1 tbsp. instant onion
¼ tsp. black pepper

The How
Crumb the bread in blender. Remove crumbs. Put spinach, cream, butter, and seasonings into container. Blend 20 seconds on high speed. Add eggs, and blend on low speed 5 seconds. Fill custard cups ¾ full and place in pan of hot water. Bake at 350° until firm. Unmold and serve with a slice of egg on top of each timbale. Pour white sauce over and sprinkle with paprika.

Corn Pudding
The What
¼ lb. fried sausage meat
3 eggs
1 tbsp. instant onion
2 tbsps. green pepper flakes
1 tbsp. pimento flakes
1 tbsp. sugar
1 tsp. lemon juice
½ tsp. salt
2 tbsps. melted butter
2 cups cream-style corn
2 cups scalded milk

The How

Put 1 cup scalded milk, 1 cup corn, and all seasonings into container. Blend on high speed 15 seconds. Add sausage meat, which has been broken up, and blend 5 seconds on high. Add eggs and blend 5 seconds on low, adding melted butter and balance of milk. Put in bowl and add balance of corn. Turn into buttered casserole and bake at 325° for 1 hour, or until well set. *Serve from casserole to 4 to 6.*

Blender Stroganoff
The What
1½ lbs. thinly sliced beef tenderloin
3 tbsps. butter
½ cup canned tomatoes
1 can mushroom soup
1 tbsp. instant onion
¼ tsp. garlic powder
¼ tsp. pepper
½ tsp. salt
½ tsp. oregano flakes
3 tbsps. flour
1 cup sour cream
2 tbsps. red wine

The How

Cut beef into thin strips and brown in butter. Cover and cook slowly for 20 minutes. Put balance of ingredients into blender and blend until smooth. Pour over beef and cook 15 minutes on low heat. Serve with sautéed mushroom caps and small boiled potatoes. *Serves 6.*

Ham Stuffed Peppers
The What
4 green peppers
2 slices bread
2 cups ground cooked ham (or chopped fine)
¾ tsp. salt
½ tsp. dry mustard
2 eggs
1 tbsp. instant onion
¼ cup parsley clusters
¼ tsp. black pepper

The How
Cut off top of green pepper. Remove seeds and white pulp. Parboil in salted water for 5 minutes and drain. Crumb bread slices in blender and remove. Put eggs, parsley, and seasonings into blender and blend for 10 seconds on high speed. Mix with crumbs and chopped ham in bowl. Stuff peppers. Put in covered baking dish and bake at 350° for 40 minutes. *Serves 4.*

Ham Soufflé
The What
1 can (4½ ozs.) deviled ham
5 eggs
1 cup hot milk
4 tbsps. soft butter
4 tbsps. flour
½ tsp. salt
¼ tsp. pepper
¼ tsp. thyme

The How
Separate eggs. Put yolks in blender with balance of ingredients. Blend on high speed 30 seconds. Cook in saucepan over low heat until thickened, stirring often. Beat egg whites stiff and fold in. Pour into deep, 1½-quart baking dish and bake in preheated 375° oven for 30 minutes. Serve at once to 4 gourmets.

Liver Loaf
The What
2 slices bread
1 medium onion
1 tbsp. tomato paste
2 large cloves garlic
½ cup parsley clusters
3 tbsps. flour
1½ tsps. salt
½ tsp. black pepper
1 tsp. oregano flakes
5 tbsps. bacon fat
1½ lbs. raw beef liver
4 slices bacon
1⅓ cups milk

The How
Crumb bread in blender and remove. Put onions, parsley, tomato paste, and garlic in blender, and blend on high for 3 seconds. Drain milk and save. Sauté chopped vegetables in 2 tablespoons bacon fat. Cut up liver, removing membrane and veins. Add to blender with milk (and milk saved from blending vegetables), sautéed onion-garlic mixture, and all seasonings. Blend on high speed 20 seconds. Mix with bread crumbs in 9″ x 5″ x 2¾″

loaf pan. Top with bacon strips and bake 1½ hours at 325°. *Serves 6 to 8.*

Mock Duck
The What
1 lb. ground pork (lean)
1 lb. ground beef round
1 lb. ground veal
dash Tabasco sauce
1 tbsp. salt
1 tsp. oregano
2 slices fresh bread, cubed
1 medium onion, cut up
½ tsp. pepper
½ cup parsley sprigs
2 eggs
¼ cup melted bacon fat or butter
¼ cup chicken stock ⎫
¼ cup orange juice ⎬ for basting

The How
Put meats in mixing bowl. Put balance of ingredients, except chicken stock and orange juice, in blender. Blend on high speed 10 seconds, and then mix with meat, thoroughly. Shape into an oval loaf and bake at 375° for 1½ hours, basting occasionally with the chicken stock and orange juice combination. *Serves 10.*

Fish Fillets Marseille
The What
6 fish fillets
1 whole ripe tomato
2 tsps. green pepper flakes

1 tbsp. instant onion
¼ tsp. tarragon flakes
1 tsp. lemon juice
2 tbsps. French dressing

The How
Blend all ingredients except fish for 10 seconds on high speed. Put each fillet on aluminum foil large enough to make an envelope. Pour sauce over each fillet. Fold and seal envelope to hold sauce in. Put envelopes on baking sheet and bake 15 minutes at 350°. *Serves 3 hungry gourmands or 6 gourmets.*

Curried Shrimp Ceylon
The What
1 lb. shrimp, shelled and deveined
¼ cup orange marmalade
2 tbsps. lemon juice
¼ tsp. powdered ginger
1 tsp. salt
1 tbsp. curry powder
½ cup water
½ cup cubed apple
1 small onion, cut up
2 tbsps. flour
½ cup cream
¼ cup seedless raisins
¼ cup blanched almonds

The How
Put all ingredients except shrimp, cream, raisins, and almonds in blender. Blend on high speed 15 seconds. Put in saucepan and stir-cook 15 minutes. Add shrimp, raisins,

Blender Specialties

and almonds. Stir-cook 10 minutes. Stir in cream. Heat and serve over hot rice. *Serves 4.*

King Crab Devils
The What
4 slices bread
1 chopped medium onion
¾ tsp. salt
¾ tsp. dry mustard
3 eggs
2 parsley clusters
1 can (6½–7 ozs.) King crab, flaked

The How
Blender crumb the bread and put into bowl. Blend balance of ingredients except crab on high speed for 10 seconds. Add crab and blend on low for 3 seconds. Pour over bread crumbs. Shape into flat cakes, roll in flour, and brown on both sides in bacon fat. Serve with tartar sauce.

Chicken Croquettes
The What
2 cups cooked chicken or turkey, finely chopped
¼ cup melted butter
½ cup cream
1 small onion, cut up
⅔ cup flour
1 stalk celery, cut up
½ tsp. salt
¼ tsp. pepper

The How
Blend all ingredients except meat on high speed for 15

seconds. Stir-cook in saucepan until thick and smooth. Mix with meat and chill. Form into cones. Roll in fine crumbs, then dip into an egg wash made by beating 1 egg with 1 tablespoon water. Roll again in crumbs and deep fry until golden brown. *Serves 6.*

Heavenly Chicken Loaf
The What
4 cups ground cooked chicken
2 cups cracker crumbs
¼ green pepper
1 canned pimento
1 tsp. salt
1 medium onion, cut up
¾ cup chicken stock
½ cup milk
3 eggs
2 tbsps. melted butter
¼ tsp. pepper
½ tsp. thyme

The How
Mix ground chicken and cracker crumbs in bowl. Blend balance of ingredients on high speed for 12 seconds. Mix well with chicken. Grease a loaf pan, 8″ x 4½″ x 2½″. Pack in chicken mixture. Place in larger pan in 1″ of hot water and bake at 350° for 1 hour. Serve with creamed mushrooms. *Serves 6.*

Chicken Velvet
The What
4½-lb. chicken, cut up
2 tbsps. cooking oil
2 tbsps. butter

½ cup canned tomato
¼ cup dry white wine
2 tbsps. chili sauce
½ tsp. garlic powder
1 medium onion, cut up
1 diced carrot
1¼ tsps. salt
¼ tsp. pepper
½ cup flour

The How
Brown chicken on all sides in oil and butter. Blend balance of ingredients on high speed for 30 seconds. Pour over chicken. Cover and simmer 40 minutes until chicken is tender. Stir now and then. *Serves 4.*

Chicken and Mushroom Casserole
The What
8-oz. pkg. noodles, cooked and drained
2 canned pimentos
3 ozs. cream cheese
1 tbsp. instant onion
1 tsp. basil flakes
1 tsp. salt
¼ tsp. pepper
pinch of nutmeg
4 tbsps. soft butter
¼ lb. mushrooms
½ cup hot milk
¾ cup diced cooked chicken

The How
Blend all ingredients except noodles and chicken for 25 seconds on high speed. Add chicken and blend 3 seconds.

Layer noodles and sauce in 1½-quart casserole. Cover and bake in preheated 350° oven for 35 minutes. *Serves 4.*
NOTE: This recipe tastes equally delicious with tuna fish, turkey, or tender pork instead of chicken.

COLD ENTREES

Shore Society Mold
The What
2 envelopes plain gelatin
6 tbsps. lemon juice
1 cup mayonnaise
½ tsp. salt
½ tsp. pepper
1 cup crab meat, shrimp, or lobster
1 cup cut-up celery
1 tsp. onion flakes
1 tbsp. parsley flakes
1 tsp. tarragon flakes
1 canned pimento

The How
Put ½ cup boiling water and 1 envelope gelatin in blender. Blend on high speed for 10 seconds. Add 4 tablespoons lemon juice, mayonnaise, and salt. Blend 10 seconds. Pour into 5-cup ring mold and chill until firm. Put second envelope of gelatin and ½ cup boiling water in blender. Blend 10 seconds. Add 1 cup water, celery, onion, parsley, tarragon, pepper, and pimento. Blend on high speed for 20 seconds. Add crab meat or other seafood and blend on low for 5 seconds. Pour on top of chilled mayonnaise mix in ring mold and chill until set. *Serves 6.*

Crab Mousse Marsala
The What
2 envelopes gelatin
2 tbsps. Marsala wine
½ cup hot ham or chicken stock
2 egg yolks
1 tsp. Worcestershire sauce
1 tsp. onion flakes or powder
½ cup mayonnaise
¼ cup chopped celery
1 tsp. parsley flakes
¼ tsp. oregano flakes
1 can (6½ ozs.) crabmeat
1 cup cream

The How
Blend gelatin, stock, and wine on high speed for 30 seconds. Add balance of ingredients except cream and crabmeat, and blend on high again 30 seconds. Add cream, blend 5 seconds. Add flaked crabmeat and blend on low speed for 10 seconds. Fold in 2 stiffly beaten egg whites and chill in mold about 2 hours. *Serves 5 to 6.*

Tuna Party Mold
The What
1 envelope plain gelatin
¼ cup tarragon vinegar
2 tbsps. parsley flakes
1 tsp. onion flakes
1 tsp. dry mustard
½ tsp. salt
¾ cup chopped celery
½ cup chopped cucumber (unpeeled)

1 cup whipping cream (whipped)
1 lb. can tuna fish

The How
Put gelatin in blender with ½ cup hot water. Blend on high speed for 20 seconds. Add vinegar, salt, mustard, onion, and parsley. Blend 30 seconds on high. Add celery and cucumber and blend 7 seconds more. Add tuna and blend 10 seconds on low speed. Pour into bowl and fold in whipped cream. Pour into mold and chill until set. *Serves 6.*

Jellied Ham Supreme
The What
½ cup bouillon
1 lb. cooked ham, diced
1 envelope plain gelatin
1 tbsp. lemon juice
½ tsp. dry mustard
1 cup chopped celery
2 tbsps. green pepper flakes
1 tsp. onion flakes
1 cup tomato juice
1 tsp. Worcestershire sauce
¼ tsp. salt

The How
Blend gelatin with hot bouillon on high speed for 10 seconds. Add balance of ingredients except ham and blend for 10 seconds. Put ham in bowl and pour blended ingredients over. Mix and chill in 4-cup mold overnight. Serve with sliced tomatoes on a bed of lettuce leaves. *Serves 6.*

Festive Ham Loaf
The What
1 envelope plain gelatin
½ cup hot bouillon
1 cup French dressing
1 tbsp. wine vinegar
1 tsp. sugar
1 tsp. salt
1 tsp. onion flakes
1 tbsp. parsley flakes
¼ cup canned mushrooms
2 stalks celery, chopped
1 lb. cooked ham, sliced thin
4 cups cooked diced potato

The How
Line a 9″ x 5″ x 3″ loaf pan with foil, letting foil extend up over sides. Cover bottom and sides with ½ of the sliced ham. Dice balance of ham. Blend gelatin and bouillon for 10 seconds on high speed. Add balance of ingredients, except ham and potatoes, and blend on high speed for 30 seconds. Mix with ham and potatoes and pack into loaf pan. Chill for 3 hours or until firm. Unmold onto cold serving platter. *Serves 6.*

Corned Beef Cones
The What
1 envelope plain gelatin
1⅓ cups hot bouillon or stock
1 tbsp. lemon juice
1 tsp. dry mustard
1 cup celery, cut up
1 tbsp. parsley flakes

12-oz. can corned beef, diced
¼ tsp. salt

The How
Blend gelatin, with ⅓ cup hot bouillon and lemon juice, on high speed for 20 seconds. Add celery, mustard, seasoning, and consommé. Blend 30 seconds on high speed. Turn to low speed and add corned beef gradually. When mixed well, place in custard cups and chill until set. Unmold on lettuce leaves. Garnish with sliced stuffed olives and radish roses. *Serves 6.*

Chicken Wonder
The What
1 envelope plain gelatin
2 tbsps. dry sherry
1 tsp. lemon juice
½ cup hot chicken stock
¼ tsp. dry mustard
¼ cup mayonnaise
2 egg yolks
1 tbsp. parsley flakes
1 tsp. onion flakes
¼ tsp. pepper
½ cup celery, finely chopped
1 cup small canned peas
2 cups diced chicken
½ cup finely chopped green pepper

The How
Blend gelatin, chicken stock, sherry, lemon juice, mustard, pepper, parsley, and onion on high speed for 30 seconds. Add egg yolks and mayonnaise and blend on low

speed for 10 seconds. Pour into bowl and fold in balance of ingredients. Rinse mold in cold water, pour in mixture, and chill until set. Serve with watercress salad. *Serves 4 or 5.*

BLENDER SOUPS

The blender excels in making pureed soups for serving hot or cold. The latitude for producing varieties of tastes and combinations is almost unlimited.

Borscht in a Hurry
The What
1½ cups sour cream
1 cup beef consommé
1 tsp. lemon juice
1 tsp. onion powder
1 cup cooked, diced beets
½ cup juice from beets
¼ cup tomato juice
1 tsp. Worcestershire sauce
1 cup crushed ice

The How
Blend all ingredients except ice on high speed for 30 seconds. Turn to low speed, add ice, and blend for 10 seconds. Serve with additional sour cream on the side for those who like it on top. *Serves 6.*

Vichyssoise
The What
1 stalk of leek (white part only)

2 tbsps. butter
1½ cups diced potato, ½" dice
1½ cups chicken broth
¼ cup diced celery, finely cut
½ tsp. salt
⅛ tsp. pepper
½ tsp. chervil flakes

The How
Slice leek and sauté in butter. Bring chicken broth to boil and add celery. Boil 5 minutes. Add potatoes, leeks with butter, and all seasonings. Boil 10 minutes. Blend on high speed for 30 seconds. If cold vichyssoise is desired, turn blender to low speed and add 1 cup crushed ice. Blend 10 seconds. Strain through coarse sieve. *Serves 5 or 6.*

Quick Cheese Soup
The What
1 can condensed cream of celery soup
½ cup Sauterne
1 cup diced cheddar cheese
⅛ tsp. garlic powder
⅛ tsp. nutmeg
1 cup whole milk

The How
Heat celery soup and milk, but do not boil. Put in blender with balance of ingredients and blend on high speed for 20 seconds. Keep hot in top of double boiler until served. *Serves 4 to 6.*

Clam Bisque
The What
2 cans (7½ ozs. each) minced clams with liquid

1 tsp. celery salt
1 tsp. Worcestershire sauce
¼ tsp. tarragon flakes
1 cup heavy cream

The How
Blend all ingredients except cream on high speed for 20 seconds. Turn to low speed, add cream, and blend for 5 more seconds. Serve hot or cold. If serving cold, add 1 cup crushed ice and blend for 5 seconds on low. *Serves 4 or 5.*

Elite Cream of Mushroom
The What
½ lb. mushrooms, sliced
¼ cup chopped onion
1 stalk celery, sliced
½ tsp. salt
1 cup chicken broth or stock
1 tbsp. sherry
⅛ tsp. pepper
½ cup heavy cream
1 tsp. Worcestershire sauce
3 tbsps. butter

The How
Sauté mushrooms, celery, and onion in butter until tender (about 8 minutes). Put in blender and add balance of ingredients except cream. Blend 30 seconds on high. Turn to low speed and add cream. Blend 5 seconds. Turn into saucepan and simmer slowly for 5 minutes until slightly thickened. *Serves 4 or 5.*

Minestrone
The What
½ cup water
2 cans (10½ ozs. consommé)
½ cup canned tomatoes
1½ cups chopped cabbage
½ tsp. garlic powder
1 tbsp. parsley flakes
2 tbsps. celery flakes
½ tsp. oregano flakes
⅛ tsp. pepper
1 can chick peas, drained
1 cup cooked macaroni

The How
Put water, tomatoes, ½ can of consommé, and all the seasonings in blender. Blend on high for 10 seconds. Add chopped cabbage and blend for 30 more seconds. Pour into saucepan and bring to boil, slowly. Simmer 10 minutes. Add macaroni and peas and simmer 5 minutes longer. Add more salt if required. Top with grated Parmesan cheese. *Serves 6.*

Cold Chicken Curry Soup
The What
1 can (10½ ozs.) cream of chicken soup
¾ tsp. curry powder
¼ tsp. Worcestershire sauce
1 cup whole milk
1 cup cracked ice

The How
Blend all ingredients except ice on high speed for 10

Blender Specialties

seconds. Turn to low speed and add ice. Blend 5 seconds. Strain through coarse sieve to remove any chunks of ice. *Serves 4.*

Oyster Bisque
The What
1 can (7 ozs.) frozen oysters, thawed
1 can (10½ ozs.) cream of celery soup
1 cup light cream
2 tbsps. dry sherry
½ tsp. tarragon flakes
½ cup chicken consommé
½ tsp. Worcestershire sauce

The How
Blend all ingredients on high speed for 20 seconds. Heat over hot water and serve to 5 or 6 epicures.

Leftover Bean Soup
The What
1 cup baked beans
2 cups chicken consommé, or stock
1 tsp. onion flakes
¼ tsp. thyme flakes
¼ cup finely chopped ham

The How
Blend all ingredients except ham on high speed for 30 seconds. Heat in saucepan and serve with chopped ham sprinkled on top of each serving. *Serves 3 or 4.*

Green Pea Supreme
The What
1 can frozen potato soup, thawed

1 #2 can green peas
½ cup chicken consommé, or broth
¼ tsp. marjoram
1 tsp. lemon juice

The How
Blend all ingredients on high speed for 20 seconds. Heat slowly, stirring, and serve to 5 or 6.

Louisiana Bisque
The What
1 can shrimp (7½ ozs.)
1 cup milk
2 tbsps. parsley flakes
½ tsp. lemon juice
½ cup light cream
¼ tsp. tarragon flakes

The How
Blend ½ the shrimp, shrimp liquid, and balance of ingredients for 20 seconds on high speed. Turn into saucepan and stir-cook until slightly thickened. Finely chop balance of shrimp and divide among servings. *Serves 4.*

Cream of Lima Bean
The What
1 #2 can lima beans
1 can chicken broth
1 tsp. onion flakes
½ tsp. marjoram flakes
1 tsp. parsley flakes
⅛ tsp. pepper

¼ tsp. salt
½ cup light cream

The How
Put all ingredients except cream in blender. Blend on high speed for 20 seconds. Turn to low, add cream, and blend for 5 seconds. Heat and serve hot topped with chopped chives. Also good served very cold. *Serves 5 or 6.*

EGG AND CHEESE DISHES

Omelets and other cheese and egg dishes have always been popular. With a blender the preparation time is cut and the texture improved. Here's the lineup of some good ones.

Blender Omelets
First, the directions for a plain omelet for 2 people.

The What
4 eggs
2 tbsps. cream (or milk)
pinch of salt, pepper, nutmeg

The How
Blend all ingredients on high speed for 3 seconds. Heat 2 tablespoons butter in about a 10″ frying pan. When butter starts to brown, pour in egg mixture and stir rapidly until it begins to set. Smooth top and cook until almost set. Put 1 tsp. butter on each of two hot serving dishes. Put half of omelet on each, upside down.

Mexican Omelet
Blend:
1 green onion, sliced
1 tbsp. green pepper flakes
4 eggs
2 slices crisp bacon
dash tabasco
⅛ tsp. salt

Cook as any omelet. *Serves 2.*

Ham Omelet
Blend:
4 eggs
4 tbsps. water
5 tbsps. chopped ham
¼ tsp. thyme
salt and pepper

Cook as any omelet. *Serves 2.*

Herb Omelet
Blend:
4 tbsps. parsley sprigs
4 tbsps. milk
1 sliced green onion
1 tsp. dry tarragon flakes
4 eggs
salt and pepper

Cook as any omelet. *Serves 2.*

Cheese Omelet
Blend:

4 tbsps. sour cream
4 eggs
4 tbsps. cheddar cheese
1 tsp. onion flakes
salt and pepper

Cook as any omelet. *Serves 2.*

Cheese Fluff Omelet
The What
6 egg yolks
1 cup diced cheddar cheese
¾ tsp. salt
¼ tsp. white pepper
⅓ cup whole milk
2 tbsps. parsley flakes
½ tsp. onion flakes

The How
Blend all ingredients on high speed for 10 seconds. Pour into greased skillet and cook covered over low heat for 5 minutes. Uncover and cook 2 minutes more. Transfer to 375° oven and brown top. *Serves 4.*

Cheese Fondue
The What
1 lb. diced Gruyere cheese (or Tilsit)
2 tsps. cornstarch
¼ tsp. pepper
dash of tabasco
1⅓ cups dry white wine, heated below boil
¼ tsp. garlic powder
2 tbsps. kirsch or dry gin

The How
Blend all ingredients except kirsch on high speed for 30 seconds. Reheat in top of double boiler over simmering water, stirring often, for 10 minutes. Add kirsch, stir in, and serve to 4 or 5 people, who will be waiting with chunks of French bread and smacking lips.

Blender Rarebit
The What
1 cup diced cheddar cheese
½ tsp. dry mustard
¼ tsp. salt
¼ tsp. pepper
1 tbsp. soft butter
⅓ cup hot milk
2 tbsps. sherry

The How
Blend all ingredients for 10 seconds on high speed. Heat in top of double boiler over simmering water. Serve to 2 over hot buttered toast.

Cheese and Bacon Puffs
The What
12 slices bacon, cooked crisp
8 slices bread
4 slices processed cheese (nippy is best)
2 cups milk
3 eggs
½ tsp. salt
¼ tsp. thyme
⅛ tsp. pepper
1 tsp. paprika
4 tbsps. diced strong cheese

The How
Make 4 sandwiches with the bacon and processed cheese slices. Cut diagonally and place in baking dish, overlapping about half. Blend balance of ingredients on high speed 15 seconds. Pour over sandwiches and let stand one half hour. Bake 30 minutes until puffed and golden, in a 350° oven. *Serves 4.*

Cheese and Onion Pie
The What
pastry to line a 9" pie plate
¼ cup diced onion
2 tbsps. butter
½ lb. mild cheddar cheese
3 eggs
½ tsp. salt
½ tsp. chervil or basil flakes
⅛ tsp. nutmeg
1 cup cream heated just under boil

The How
Line pie plate with pastry. Prick pastry to prevent puffing. Put another pie plate in on top of pastry. Bake 8 minutes in preheated 400° oven. Sauté onions in butter, and sprinkle into pastry, after it is cooled. Blend balance of ingredients on high speed for 20 seconds. Pour into pastry and bake 35 minutes in a preheated 350° oven until set. *Serves 6.*

VEGETABLE DISHES

These tasty dishes are all prepared in a hurry and combine good appearance with gourmet flavor.

Potato Pudding
The What
4 medium potatoes, diced
½ cup diced onion
3 eggs
2 tbsps. parsley flakes
¼ tsp. pepper
1 tsp. salt
½ tsp. celery flakes
½ cup flour
¼ cup soft butter
½ cup milk

The How
Blend potatoes and onion (only until just chopped—do not puree) with a little water and drain in sieve. Put balance of ingredients in blender and blend on high speed for 10 seconds. Mix with vegetables and put in greased casserole. Bake in preheated 350° oven for 1 hour. *Serves 4 to 5.*

Corn Fritters
The What
1 cup fresh, frozen, or canned corn
1 egg
½ tsp. salt
¼ cup flour
¼ cup milk
pinch of nutmeg

The How
Blend all ingredients on high speed for 15 seconds. Drop batter by spoonfuls into hot fat at least one inch deep. Fry until lightly browned. *Makes 1 dozen small fritters.*

Sweet Potato Poem
The What
seeded pulp of 2 oranges
4 cooked and mashed sweet potatoes (4 cups)
¼ cup melted butter
½ tsp. salt
¼ cup milk
3 tbsps. brown sugar
2 tbsps. sweet or medium sherry
¼ tsp. nutmeg
3 thin strips orange peel
1 tsp. lemon juice

The How
Blend all ingredients except potatoes on high speed for 30 seconds. Turn to low speed and drop in potatoes until mixture gets too thick to blend well. Pour into any mashed potatoes you have left, and mix thoroughly. Put in buttered casserole and bake in preheated 350° oven 35 minutes.

Spanish Rice Ring
The What
1 can (16 ozs.) tomatoes
½ cup sharp cheddar cheese, diced
¼ tsp. garlic powder
2 tbsps. green pepper flakes, or 1 pepper
½ tsp. dry mustard
½ tsp. white pepper
1 tsp. salt
2 tbsps. instant onion, or flakes
¼ cup melted butter
4½ cups cooked rice
½ tsp. oregano flakes

The How
Blend all ingredients except rice on high speed for 20 seconds. Mix with rice. Pack into greased 1½-quart ring mold. Bake in a pan of hot water in 350° oven for 75 minutes. Fill center of ring with creamed vegetables. *Serves 6.*

Corn Pie
The What
1½ slices bread
¾ cup diced sharp cheddar cheese
3 eggs
½ tsp. salt
1½ cups kernel corn niblets
3 tbsps. soft butter
1 tbsp. parsley flakes
1 tsp. sugar
1 tsp. onion flakes
pastry for 9″ pie shell

The How
Blend 1½ slices bread and the cheese on low speed until crumbed and mixed. Pour out and reserve. Line pie shell with pastry, making a standing fluted edge. Blend balance of ingredients on high speed 20 seconds. Mix in bread crumbs and cheese. Pour into shell and bake 10 minutes in preheated 450° oven. Turn heat to 350° and bake 30 minutes more. *Serves 5 or 6.*

Puffed Spud Casserole
The What
1 cup diced mild cheddar cheese
½ cup milk

Blender Specialties

3 eggs
1 tbsp. parsley flakes
1 tsp. onion flakes
1 tbsp. green pepper flakes
1½ tsps. salt
¼ tsp. black pepper
¼ cup melted butter
1½ cups diced raw potatoes

The How
Blend all ingredients on high speed for 20 seconds. Pour into buttered 1½-quart casserole and bake at 350° for 1 hour. *Serves 6.*

Zingy Beets
The What
3 cups sliced cooked beets
½ cup diced cooked beets
3 tbsps. cider vinegar
1 tsp. onion flakes
1 tsp. parsley flakes
⅛ tsp. ground cloves
¼ cup white sugar
2 tbsps. soft butter

The How
Put all ingredients except the sliced beets into blender. Blend on high speed for 10 seconds. Put sliced beets into saucepan and pour on sauce from blender. Simmer slowly, stirring often, for 10 to 15 minutes. *Serves 4 to 5.*

Vegetable Custard
The What
2 cups mixed carrots and peas

3 eggs
¼ cup milk
1 tbsp. instant onion flakes or diced onion
2 tbsps. parsley flakes
2 tbsps. flour
3 tbsps. soft butter
1 tsp. salt
¼ tsp. pepper
½ tsp. Worcestershire sauce

The How
Blend all ingredients on high speed for 10 seconds. Pour into buttered custard cups. Place cups in pan with 1 inch of water and bake 50 minutes in preheated 350° oven. Serve garnished with celery and carrot sticks. *Serves 6.*

Cornfield Casserole
The What
10 soda crackers
1 tbsp. Roquefort cheese (optional)
16-oz. can cream-style corn
2 tbsps. green pepper flakes
1 tbsp. instant onion flakes
½ tsp. marjoram flakes
2 tbsps. soft butter

The How
Blender crumb the soda crackers. Remove and toss with soft butter until well mixed. Blend half the corn with balance of ingredients on high speed for 20 seconds. Mix well with balance of corn and put in buttered casserole. Top with buttered crumbs. Bake uncovered 45 minutes in preheated 325° oven. *Serves 4 to 6.*

Rice and Lima Casserole
The What
- 2 cups cooked lima beans
- 2 cups cooked rice (instant, prepared)
- 4 tbsps. celery flakes
- 1 tsp. green pepper flakes
- 1 tsp. instant onion
- 1½ cups tomato juice
- 2 tbsps. soft butter
- 1 tsp. salt
- ¼ tsp. pepper
- 1 tsp. lemon juice

The How

Mix rice and beans in buttered casserole. Blend balance of ingredients for 20 seconds on high speed. Pour over rice and beans. Bake 30 minutes in preheated 350° oven. *Serves 4.* NOTE: For a gourmet touch, butter 1 cup bread crumbs, mix in ¼ cup grated cheese of your choice, and use as a topping.

SAUCES

The blender takes all the tedium out of preparing sauces. Sauces for dishes that are to be baked can be prepared in the blender and can be poured over or mixed into the dish without pre-cooking—a great saving in time and effort. Blender prepared sauces are smoother than sauces prepared any other way.

Basic Medium Cream Sauce
The What
- 4 tbsps. flour

4 tbsps. soft butter or margarine
½ tsp. salt
¼ tsp. pepper
2 cups hot whole milk

The How
Put 1 cup hot milk in blender and turn on low speed. Add flour slowly, then butter and seasonings. Add balance of milk and blend on high speed for 10 seconds. Stir-cook over low heat 3 minutes after sauce starts to bubble.

Thin Sauce
Use 2 tablespoons flour and 2 tablespoons butter in above recipe.

Thick Sauce
Use 6 tablespoons flour and 6 tablespoons butter in basic recipe.

Chicken à la King Sauce
The What
1 cup basic white sauce
½ cup cream
1 sliced canned pimento
¼ tsp. thyme
1 tsp. instant onion
1 tbsp. sherry

The How
Blend all ingredients on high speed for 10 seconds. Heat to slow bubble, stirring, and add chicken.

Blender Zip Sauce
For asparagus, fish or veal.

The What
1 cup hot medium white sauce
1½ cups mayonnaise
1 tbsp. lemon juice
3 dashes Tabasco
¼ tsp. white pepper

The How
Blend all ingredients on low speed until mixed, then 3 seconds on high speed. *Makes 2½ cups.*

Creole Sauce
The What
1 cup hot basic white sauce, medium
6 tbsps. tomato sauce
2 tbsps. celery flakes
2 tbsps. green pepper flakes
2 tbsps. instant minced onion
¼ tsp. salt
¼ tsp. pepper
¼ tsp. oregano

The How
Blend all ingredients on high speed for 10 seconds. Use wherever Sauce Creole is called for.

Poulette Sauce
The What
1 cup basic thick white sauce
1 cup chicken broth
1 tbsp. parsley flakes
¼ tsp. lemon juice
1 tbsp. flour
1 tbsp. soft butter

The How
Blend all ingredients on low speed for 20 seconds. Stir cook slowly 5 minutes.

Mushroom Sauce
The What
1 cup thick white sauce
1 can (4 ozs.) mushrooms with juice
½ tsp. Worcestershire sauce

The How
Blend ingredients on high speed for 5 seconds. *Makes 1½ cups.*

Sauce Mornay
The What
1 cup hot medium white sauce
2 tbsps. diced Gruyere cheese
2 tbsps. grated Parmesan cheese
2 tbsps. soft butter

The How
Blend all ingredients on high speed for 10 seconds. Reheat over hot water, stir, and serve.

Farmdale Chicken Sauce
The What
1 can condensed cream of chicken soup
¼ cup coffee cream
2 tbsps. parsley flakes
¼ tsp. garlic powder

The How
Blend all ingredients on high speed for 10 seconds. Stir-

cook to boiling and ½ minute after boiling. A great sauce for roast or fried chicken.

Butter Sauce
Excellent on fish, asparagus, spinach, or green beans.

The What
½ cup soft butter
1 tbsp. lemon juice
1½ tbsps. grated lemon rind
¼ cup chicken bouillon
1 tbsp. chive or dill flakes
½ cup grated cheese of your choice—sharp cheddar, Romano, or Parmesan

The How
Blend all ingredients on high speed for 10 seconds. Reheat over hot water and serve.

Cheese Sauce (*Au Gratin*)
The What
1 can (10½ ozs.) condensed cream of celery soup
¼ cup milk
1 tsp. instant onion
2 dashes Tabasco
½ cup diced strong cheddar cheese
1 tbsp. soft butter
½ tsp. paprika

The How
Blend all ingredients on high speed for 20 seconds. Heat to serving temperature.

Waterfowl Sauce
Adds zest to duck, goose, or guinea hen.

The What
2 tbsps. lemon juice
2 tbsps. thin slices orange rind
¼ cup sherry
½ cup currant jelly
¼ cup orange juice
1 tsp. dry mustard
1 tsp. cornstarch
½ tsp. Worcestershire sauce

The How
Blend all ingredients on high speed for 20 seconds. Stir and simmer for 5 minutes. Serve hot over fowl slices.

Honey Mayonnaise
The What
1 cup mayonnaise
2 tbsps. honey
¼ tsp. ginger
1 tsp. lemon juice
2 drops red food color

The How
Blend all ingredients on low speed for 30 seconds. Excellent on fruit salads.

Curry Mayonnaise
For fish or lamb patties.

The What
1 cup mayonnaise
1 tsp. lime juice
1 tsp. curry powder

¼ tsp. garlic powder
2 tbsps. honey
½ tsp. onion flakes or powder
¼ tsp. ginger

The How
Blend all ingredients on low speed for 30 seconds.

Hollandaise-in-a-Minute
The What
½ cup butter, hot
2 eggs
2 tbsps. lemon juice
¼ tsp. salt
dash Tabasco

The How
Blend all ingredients except butter on low speed. Then add hot butter with blender running. Keep warm over warm water until serving.

Thousand Island Sauce
The What
1 cup mayonnaise
¼ cup chili sauce
4 sweet gherkins
2 tbsps. parsley flakes
1 tsp. green pepper
1 tsp. instant onion
1 tsp. celery flakes
¼ cup stuffed olives
1 tsp. paprika
1 hard-boiled egg

The How
Blend all ingredients on low speed for 10 seconds and on high 5 seconds. Serve over lettuce or other salad greens.

Sauce Aioli
Blend 2 teaspoons garlic powder into 1 cup mayonnaise. Serve with grilled lamb or other meats to garlic lovers. This is what breath sweetness is all about!

Sauce Bearnaise
For broiled steak or other meats.

The What
3 tbsps. white wine
1 tbsp. tarragon flakes
1 tbsp. chopped shallots (or onion)
1 tbsp. vinegar
¼ tsp. black pepper
¾ cup blender Hollandaise

The How
Put all ingredients except Hollandaise in saucepan. Cook slowly until liquid is almost gone. Pour into blender. Add Hollandaise and blend on high speed for 5 seconds. Reheat and serve.

Sauce Tartare
The What
1¼ cups mayonnaise
5 sweet gherkins
3 pitted olives
1 tsp. tarragon flakes
1 tsp. parsley flakes
¼ tsp. black pepper

Blender Specialties

The How
Blend on high speed for 7 seconds. Stir down and blend on low speed for 5 seconds.

Barbecue Sauce
For Meat or Chicken.

The What
1 cup chili sauce
½ cup red wine
½ tsp. garlic powder
1 egg
3 tbsps. lemon juice
¼ cup salad oil
1 tsp. salt
1 tsp. dry mustard
½ tsp. white pepper
2 tbsps. Worcestershire sauce
3 tbsps. sugar
1 tsp. oregano flakes
1 tsp. instant onion

The How
Put egg and lemon juice in blender. Blend on low speed for 5 seconds. Add balance of ingredients and blend on high speed for 20 seconds.

Basting Sauce
For the barbecue, snappy and flavorful.

The What
⅓ cup cider vinegar
2 tbsps. dark molasses

3 tbsps. honey
1 tsp. garlic powder
1 tbsp. Worcestershire sauce
1 tsp. salt
1 tsp. onion powder
¼ cup brown sugar
2 tbsps. lemon juice
1 tsp. dry mustard
1 tsp. oregano flakes

The How
Blend all ingredients on high speed for 30 seconds.

Pesto Italiano
Delicious with spaghetti or noodles.

The What
2 tbsps. tomato paste
½ cup olive oil
2 tbsps. parsley flakes
2 tbsps. green pepper flakes
1 tsp. garlic powder
½ tsp. salt
1 tbsp. grated Parmesan cheese
½ cup walnuts

The How
Blend all ingredients on high speed for 20 seconds. Reheat and serve over spaghetti or noodles.

Sudden Meat Sauce
The What
½ lb. ground beef

¼ lb. ground pork
1 tbsp. olive oil
2 tbsps. parsley flakes
½ tsp. garlic powder
1 tsp. salt
¼ tsp. cayenne pepper
2 tbsps. celery flakes
2 tbsps. green pepper flakes
½ tbsp. oregano flakes
1½ cups canned tomato
4 tbsps. tomato paste
¼ cup grated Parmesan cheese
1 tbsp. onion flakes

The How
Brown beef and pork in olive oil until all browned, breaking up to cook thoroughly. Put in blender with balance of ingredients. Blend on high speed for 30 seconds. Simmer slowly 10 minutes and serve over spaghetti.

SANDWICH SPREADS

The blender allows you to use your imagination in combining a variety of ingredients for inspirational spreads. Here are a number of the more popular combinations.

Date Nut Spread
The What
½ cup nut meats
pulp from 1 orange, seeded
¼ cup pineapple juice
¾ cup pitted dates

3 thin strips orange rind
1 tsp. lemon juice

The How
Blend orange pulp and pineapple juice on high speed for 5 seconds. Add balance of ingredients and blend for 20 seconds, stopping to stir down when necessary. Chill before using.

Marmalade Nut Spread
The What
3 tbsps. orange juice
¾ cup orange marmalade
6 ozs. cream cheese
¾ cup blanched almonds
2 tbsps. Grenadine

The How
Blend all ingredients on high speed for 20 seconds. Chill before using.

Deviled Ham Paste
The What
1 can (4½ ozs.) deviled ham, warmed
1 tsp. parsley flakes
1 tsp. Worcestershire sauce
2 tbsps. tomato paste
1 tbsp. tomato juice
½ tsp. onion powder
1 tbsp. celery flakes

The How
Blend on high speed for 30 seconds. Stop to stir down if necessary. Chill before using.

Egg Spread
The What
2 tbsps. mayonnaise
2 tbsps. warmed cream
¼ tsp. onion powder or flakes
½ tsp. salt
½ tsp. Worcestershire sauce
4 hard-boiled eggs

The How
Blend all ingredients except eggs on high speed for 30 seconds. Blend in egg yolks. Turn to low speed and add egg whites. Run blender until whites are just chopped.

Crab Meat Spread
The What
1 can (6½ ozs.) crabmeat
½ cup mayonnaise
1 tsp. lime juice
1 tbsp. chive flakes
¼ tsp. salt
⅛ tsp. pepper
1 tbsp. sherry

The How
Blend all ingredients except crab on high speed for 10 seconds. Drain, flake, and remove any cartilage from crab. Start blender on low speed and add crabmeat. Stop when well blended.

Chicken Liver Spread
The What
2 tbsps. bacon fat

¾ lb. chicken livers
1 tsp. onion powder
½ cup chicken broth
½ tsp. curry powder
½ tsp. salt
1 tbsp. Worcestershire sauce
¼ cup soft butter
¼ tsp. thyme

The How
Sauté chicken livers in bacon fat until lightly browned on all sides (about 10 minutes). Put in blender with heated chicken broth and blend on high speed for 15 seconds. Stop blender. Add balance of ingredients and blend on high speed for 30 seconds. Chill before using.
NOTE: For a switch in flavor, use only ½ lb. chicken livers and add ½ lb. cream cheese instead of butter.

Tuna Spread
The What
1 can (7½ ozs.) tuna, drained
½ cup mayonnaise
1 tsp. lemon juice
1 stalk celery, cut up
1 small carrot, cut up
1 tsp. Worcestershire sauce
½ tsp. salt
¼ tsp. black pepper
½ tsp. onion powder, or flakes
1 tbsp. tomato juice

The How
Blend all ingredients except tuna on high speed for 20

seconds. Turn to low speed and add tuna. Blend just until tuna is well mixed in. Chill before using.

Zippy Cheese Spread
The What
1 cup diced sharp cheddar cheese
½ cup cream
⅛ tsp. garlic powder
2 tbsps. parsley flakes
1 tsp. Worcestershire Sauce
dash of Tabasco

The How
Cover and blend all ingredients on high speed for 15 seconds. Scrape down from sides and blend 10 seconds more.

Sardine Spread
The What
1 can sardines, drained
2 tbsps. mayonnaise
2 tsps. lemon juice
½ tsp. onion flakes

The How
Blend all ingredients for 5 seconds on low speed, then 10 seconds on high speed.

Mushroom Butter
The What
½ lb. mushrooms
¼ cup butter
1 tsp. lemon juice

¼ tsp. fresh black pepper
¼ tsp. salt
3 tbsps. sherry
½ cup soft butter

The How
Sprinkle lemon juice on mushrooms, then sauté in ¼ cup butter. Put mushrooms and pan juices in blender. Blend on high speed for 10 seconds. Add balance of ingredients and blend on low speed for 20 seconds. Chill before using.

Watercress Butter
The What
1 bunch watercress (chopped)
½ cup melted butter
1 tbsp. lemon juice
¼ tsp. salt
¼ tsp. pepper

The How
Blend all ingredients on high speed for 20 seconds. Stop, stir down, and blend for 10 seconds more.

Nut Butter
The What
¾ cup walnuts or pecan halves
½ cup melted butter
¼ tsp. salt
¼ tsp. basil flakes
⅛ tsp. pepper

The How
Turn blender on low and pour in nuts. When chopped,

add balance of ingredients and blend on high speed for 10 seconds.

Lobster Butter
The What
½ cup flaked lobster meat
2 ozs. lobster paste
½ cup soft butter
¼ tsp. thyme
¼ tsp. white pepper
¼ tsp. salt
1 tbsp. lemon juice

The How
Blend all ingredients on high speed for 20 seconds. Stir down and blend for 10 more seconds. Chill before serving. A great spread for hors d'oeuvres—on crackers or small toast rounds.

BLENDER SALAD DRESSINGS AND SALADS

The blender excels in making velvet-smooth, perfectly blended salad dressings and in refining various salad ingredients.

Basic French Dressing
The What
½ cup wine vinegar or lemon juice
1 egg white
1 tsp. salt
¼ tsp. coarse black pepper
½ tsp. dry mustard

The How
Blend for 5 seconds on low speed, then 5 more seconds on high speed.

Creamy French
The What
¼ cup wine vinegar
⅛ tsp. garlic powder
1 tsp. dry mustard
1 egg white
½ tsp. salt
1 tsp. tomato paste
½ tsp. tarragon flakes
2 tbsps. mayonnaise
1 tbsp. sugar
¾ cup olive oil

The How
Blend all ingredients on high speed for 15 seconds.

Low-Calorie Dream
The What
2 green onions, chopped
3 tbsps. lemon juice
½ tsp. sugar
½ tsp. salt
1 tsp. paprika
½ tsp. garlic powder
4 radishes
1 tbsp. green pepper flakes

The How
Blend, covered, on high for 15 seconds.

Blue Cheese Dressing
The What
¾ cup french dressing
½ cup crumbled blue cheese
½ tsp. dry mustard
¼ cup dairy sour cream
¼ tsp. onion powder

The How
Blend all ingredients on low speed for 10 seconds and on high for 5.

Herbed Dressing
The What
1 cup French dressing
2 tbsps. parsley flakes
½ tsp. tarragon flakes, or dill, oregano, or marjoram

The How
Blend on high speed for 5 seconds. Let stand overnight to develop flavor.

Dressing Vincenzo
The What
1 cup French dressing
1 canned pimento
6 stalks watercress
2 green onions with tops
3 tbsps. chili sauce

The How
Blend on high speed for 30 seconds.

Ketchup Dressing
The What
1 cup ketchup
½ cup cider-vinegar
1 egg white
1 tsp. salt
¼ tsp. pepper
¾ cup salad oil
¼ tsp. garlic powder

The How
Blend on high speed for 20 seconds. Good in meat salads or egg salad.

Kong Loo Dressing
The What
½ cup canned tomato, drained
1 small onion, quartered
¼ tsp. curry powder
1 tsp. dried mint
2 tbsps. wine vinegar
1 tbsp. sugar
½ tsp. salt
¼ cup olive or salad oil

The How
Blend all ingredients on high speed for 15 seconds. This dressing is wonderful on head lettuce or carrot and cabbage slaw.

Dressing Artur
A fine general dressing.

The What
2 ozs. wine or cider vinegar

1 egg
¼ tsp. garlic powder
2 tbsps. sugar
7 ozs. salad oil
1 tsp. dry mustard
¼ tsp. black pepper
1 tsp. salt

The How
Put vinegar in blender. Add egg. Blend on low speed for 5 seconds. Start dribbling in oil until mixture starts to thicken. Add sugar and seasonings and balance of oil. If mixture becomes too thick to blend add water, 1 tablespoon at a time, until dressing is blended. This is a basic dressing to which you can add curry, tarragon, tomato paste, blue cheese, or any other flavor that suits your fancy.

Vinaigrette Dressing
The What
1 cup French dressing
6 stuffed olives
2 tbsps. green onion flakes
½ tsp. onion powder
1 tbsp. parsley flakes
1 tbsp. capers

The How
Blend for 6 or 7 seconds on high.

French Fruit Dressing
The What
⅓ cup lemon juice
2 thin strips lemon peel

½ tsp. dry mustard
2 tbsps. sugar
½ tsp. salt
pinch of garlic powder
1 tsp. paprika
1 cup salad oil

The How
Blend on high speed for 15 seconds. Excellent on fresh fruit.

Cucumber Sour Low Calorie
The What
1 cup cottage cheese
¼ cup water
2 tbsps. lemon juice
½ tsp. salt
½ tsp. sugar
1 cup diced cucumber
¼ tsp. garlic powder
1 tbsp. parsley flakes
1 dash Tabasco

The How
Blend all ingredients on high speed for 20 seconds.

Ruby Jewel Salad
The What
1 pkg. raspberry gelatin
1¼ cups boiling water
1 orange, seeded and cut up
1 can cranberry sauce

Blender Specialties

The How
Blend gelatin and hot water for 15 seconds on high speed. Add orange and cranberry sauce and blend for 15 seconds on high speed. Pour into mold and chill until firm.

Cottage Cheese Superba
The What
2 cups minced cucumber
½ cup green pepper, diced fine
¼ cup thinly sliced green onion
1 envelope plain gelatin
½ tsp. salt
½ cup boiling water
2 cups cottage cheese
1 tbsp. horseradish
½ cup coffee cream

The How
Put cucumber, green pepper, and onion in mixing bowl. Put gelatin and boiling water in blender and blend on high speed for 15 seconds. Add cottage cheese and horseradish and blend for 15 seconds. Add cream and blend for 3 seconds. Mix with vegetables. Turn into mold and chill until set. Serve on lettuce or salad greens with Creamy French Dressing. *Serves 6.*

Perfection Mold
The What
1 pkg. lemon gelatin
1 cup boiling water
1 cup sliced carrot
1 cup sliced cabbage
1 cup pineapple juice

½ tsp. salt
1 tbsp. lemon juice

The How
Blend gelatin and hot water for 15 seconds on high speed. Add balance of ingredients and blend just until last of vegetables goes down into blades. Pour into mold and chill. Serve on crisp greens. *Serves 6.*

Luau Salad
The What
1 cup crushed pineapple, drained
¼ cup chopped maraschino cherries
½ cup finely chopped celery
½ cup coarsely chopped nuts
1 pkg. lemon flavored gelatin
1 envelope plain gelatin
½ cup hot pineapple juice
3 tbsps. salad oil
1 tbsp. lemon juice
¼ tsp. salt
8 ozs. soft cream cheese

The How
Combine pineapple, cherries, celery, and nuts in mixing bowl. Put gelatin and pineapple juice in blender. Blend on high speed for 20 seconds. Add oil, lemon juice, salt, and cream cheese. Blend for 10 seconds. Add 2 heaping cups crushed ice. Blend for 20 seconds. Mix with fruit and nuts. Pour into mold and chill.

Deviled Egg
The What
1 envelope plain gelatin

½ cup hot chicken stock
½ tsp. salt
2 tbsps. lemon juice
1 tsp. Worcestershire sauce
¾ cup mayonnaise
½ tsp. onion powder
1 tbsp. green pepper flakes
1 tbsp. celery flakes
⅛ tsp. cayenne
1 tsp. paprika
4 hard-boiled eggs

The How
Blend gelatin and hot stock on high speed for 20 seconds. Add balance of ingredients except eggs and blend for 15 seconds. Put in egg yolks and blend for 5. Add egg whites and blend just until whites go down into blades. Pour into mold and chill until set. *Serves 4.*

DESSERTS

The blender can help you produce fabulous desserts—and in just minutes.

Chocolate Bavarian Cream
The What
2 envelopes plain gelatin
½ cup hot, strong coffee
¼ cup cold water
6 ozs. semi-sweet chocolate bits
2 egg yolks
1 cup cream
1 cup crushed ice

The How
Put coffee and water in blender. Add gelatin and blend on high speed for 20 seconds. Add chocolate and blend for 10 seconds. Add egg yolks and cream and blend for 10 seconds. Add crushed ice and blend on low until ice is melted. Pour into small individual molds or one 4-cup mold. Chill until set. Serve with whipped cream with 1 chocolate Maple Bud on top. *Serves 6.*

Strawberry Bavarian
The What
1 pkg. frozen strawberries, defrosted
½ cup of juice from strawberries
¼ cup milk
2 envelopes plain gelatin
¼ cup sugar
2 egg yolks
1 cup cream
1 heaping cup crushed ice

The How
Heat strawberry juice. Put milk in blender, then gelatin, and start blender on low speed. Pour in hot strawberry juice. Blend on high speed for 10 seconds, add sugar, strawberries, and egg yolks, and blend for 20 more. Add cream and ice and blend on low for 20 seconds, then on high for 10. Pour into molds of your choice and chill until set. *Serves 6.*

Blancmange
The What
¼ cup cornstarch
¼ cup sugar

¼ tsp. salt
1 tbsp. soft butter
1 strip thin lemon peel
½ cup blanched almonds
1 tsp. lemon juice
3 cups milk
½ tsp. vanilla

The How
Blend all ingredients except almonds, milk, and vanilla on high speed for 20 seconds. Add almonds and milk and blend for 15 seconds on high speed. Cook in saucepan over medium heat, stirring often. When well thickened, cool to lukewarm and stir in vanilla. Rinse molds in cold water and pour in blancmange. Chill until firm. Serve with any fruit sauce you fancy. *Serves 6.*

Maple Custard
The What
3 tbsps. maple syrup
¾ cup milk
1 egg
2 tbsps. sugar
½ tsp. vanilla
⅛ tsp. salt

The How
Coat the inside of 3 custard cups with maple syrup. Blend balance of ingredients on high speed for 4 seconds. Pour into custard cups. Set cups in 1 inch of hot water in baking dish. Bake at 325° 20 to 30 minutes until set. *Serves 3, double recipe for 6.*

Western Apple Crisp
The What
1 quart sliced apples
1 tsp. cinnamon
½ tsp. nutmeg
1 cup brown sugar
6 slices bread
1 cup diced sharp cheddar
2 tbsps. butter

The How
Crumb bread in blender on low speed. Add cheese and blend on low speed until well mixed. Mix in bowl with balance of ingredients except butter. Put in buttered baking dish, dot with butter, and bake at 350° about 40 minutes until top is crisp and brown. Serve with thick cream or soft ice cream. *Serves 6.*

Instant Charlotte Russe
The What
1 pkg. strawberry gelatin
½ cup hot orange juice
1 heaping cup crushed ice
1 cup whipping cream
2 lady fingers

The How
Blend gelatin and orange juice on high speed for 10 seconds. Add ice and cream. Blend on high for 15 seconds. Pour into molds until set (5 minutes). Top with ½ lady finger. *Serves 4.*

Cocktail Velvet
The What
1 can (1 lb.) fruit cocktail, drained
1 envelope plain gelatin
syrup from fruit

The How
Heat ¼ cup of syrup and blend with gelatin for 20 seconds. Add half the fruit and balance of syrup. Blend for 10 seconds on high speed. Add balance of fruit and blend for 5 more seconds until just chopped.

Rosy Applesauce
Makes friends of your small fry.

The What
½ cup pineapple juice
1 tsp. lemon juice
3 tbsps. red cinnamon candies
2 large tart apples, unpeeled, diced

The How
Blend pineapple juice, lemon juice, and candies on high speed for 10 seconds. Add diced apples and blend on high speed for 15 more. If serving to youngsters, add 1 cup soft ice cream and blend in. You'll be a hit with them.

Ocean Foam
The What
1 pkg. lime gelatin
½ cup hot pineapple juice
2 cups crushed ice

The How
Blend gelatin and juice for 20 seconds on high speed. Add ice and blend for 30 seconds more. Pour into mold or molds and chill until firm. *Serves 4.*

Frozen Fruit Cream
(Strawberry, Raspberry, Peach)

The What
1 pkg. frozen fruit, cut in chunks
1 tsp. lemon juice
⅔ cup evaporated milk

The How
Put in blender. Cover and blend on high speed for 30 seconds, or until smooth. *Makes 1 pint.*

Jiffy Cheese Pie
The What
1 crumb crust in 8″ pie plate
2 envelopes plain gelatin
juice of ½ lemon peel
few slivers of lemon peel
¼ cup sugar
2 eggs
½ cup hot milk
8 ozs. soft cream cheese
1 heaping cup crushed ice
1 cup whipping cream

The How
Blend milk, gelatin, lemon juice, and lemon peel on high speed for 30 seconds. Shut off. Add sugar, eggs, and cream

cheese. Blend for 10 seconds on low speed and 10 seconds on high. Add ice and cream and blend on high speed for 20 seconds. Pour into pie shell and it's ready to serve in ten minutes.

Orange Sauce
The What
1 cup orange juice
thin rind from ½ orange
¼ tsp. salt
½ cup sugar
2 tbsps. cornstarch

The How
Blend on high speed for 20 seconds. Stir-cook until thickened. *Makes 1 cup.*

Instant Chocolate Sauce
The What
1 pkg. (6 ozs.) semi-sweet chocolate
¼ cup hot coffee

The How
Blend on high speed for 20 seconds.

Lemon Sauce
The What
juice of 1 lemon
1 tbsp. thin lemon peel
2 tbsps. cornstarch
½ cup sugar
dash of salt, nutmeg
2 tbsps. butter

The How
Blend on high speed for 20 seconds. Stir-cook until thickened and clear.

MAKING BABY FOODS

A blender easily prepares fruits, meats, or vegetables into a puree for baby feeding. The saving in money is very considerable. You can prepare foods to the exact consistency required for the age of your child.

Baby Dinner De Luxe
In this recipe you can use leftover cooked meat or fish— or a combination.

The What
¼ cup cooked carrots
¼ cup cooked potato
½ cooked onion
½ cup cooked meat, or fish or liver
6 tbsps. hot tomato juice, broth, or formula

The How
Blend all ingredients together, adding more liquid if necessary to get desired consistency for feeding.

BLENDED FRUITS

You can blend fresh, cooked, or thawed frozen fruits very simply, remembering you must have some liquid to blend properly.

Banana
3 tbsps. pineapple juice
1 sliced banana

Apricot
3 tbsps. orange juice
½ cup stoned apricots
1 tbsp. honey

Peach
2 tbsps. pineapple or orange juice
½ cup diced, peeled peach

Prune
1 tsp. lemon juice
6 tsps. prune juice
½ cup pitted prunes
If dried prunes are used, soak before pitting and blending.

VEGETABLES FOR BABY

Cook in small amount of water until just tender. Blend vegetables with cooking water and a little butter. Meal quantities might be as follows:
¾ cup sliced asparagus
¾ cup Lima beans
¾ cup sliced green beans
1 cup shredded cabbage
1 cup cauliflower flowerets
¾ cup diced sweet potato
¾ cup mixed diced carrots and peas
¼ cup beet greens with ½ cup cauliflower
¼ cup sweet potato with ½ cup shredded cabbage

MEAT AND VEGETABLE DINNERS

Beef Dinner
The What
½ cup tomato juice
1 small slice onion
4 ozs. lean hamburger
½ cup sliced green beans
1 sprig parsley

The How
Blend on high speed 1 minute. Cook, stirring, 7 minutes.

Liver
The What
¼ cup tomato juice
1 slice onion
4 ozs. diced raw liver
1 cup spinach leaves
¼ tsp. celery salt

The How
Blend all ingredients on high speed 1 minute. Stir-cook 6 to 7 minutes.

Chicken
The What
¼ cup milk
1 tbsp. chopped celery, or leaves
½ cup green peas, raw or fresh frozen
1 tbsp. chopped green onion
1 pinch celery salt
4 ozs. diced raw chicken

The How
Blend on high speed 1 minute. Stir-cook 5 minutes.

NOTE
Cooked left-over meats may be used, with a few tablespoons of broth added when blending.

7. Suddenly French

While we do not intend to scoff at Escoffier, we have arrived, through research and testing, at many shortcuts that take the tedium out of French cookery, at the same time retaining the appearance and flavor of the products.

Cordon Bleu cuisine no longer means endless labor, due to the availability of frozen, precooked, freeze-dried, and preserved foods and seasonings. The modern French chef takes full advantage of the convenience ingredients, so who are we to fight culinary progress? Follow the easy steps to French gourmet cooking carefully, and these creations will make you famous in your circle of discerning friends.

APPETIZERS

Quiche Lorraine
Ham, cheese, and egg custard pie.

The What
1 pie crust mix

¼ lb. shredded boiled ham
4 eggs
2 egg yolks
4 tbsps. grated Parmesan cheese
½ cup coffee cream
½ tsp. salt
⅛ tsp. black pepper
¼ tsp. thyme

The How
Prepare pastry as directed and line a 9″ pie pan. Bake 5 minutes at 475° and cool. Spread shredded ham on crust. Mix the balance of ingredients in a bowl and beat well to mix thoroughly. Pour into crust and bake 40 minutes at 300°. If custard is set, pie is done. Serve at once to 6.
NOTE: You may substitute ½ cup diced cooked bacon for ham. In this case, add 1 tablespoon bacon fat to custard for extra flavor.

Pâté Maison
A delicious pâté of jellied liver sausage and mushrooms that tastes as though it took hours to prepare.

The What
1 lb. liverwurst
4 ozs. button mushrooms
¾ cup chicken broth, canned
1½ ozs. brandy
1 tbsp. (1 envelope) plain gelatin

The How
Slice the mushrooms and marinate in brandy for 12 hours. Then put broth in pan and heat. Add gelatin and stir

until dissolved. Do not boil. Mash liverwurst in bowl, add broth, and beat together well. Add mushroom-brandy mixture, reserving ¼ of the mushrooms, and mix well. Chill in refrigerator. When just set, beat lightly and put in oiled mold. Chill until set. After molding decorate with reserved mushroom slices. NOTE: Black olives, sliced, can be substituted for mushrooms, if you prefer them.

Caviar Blini
Wafer pancakes with caviar.

The What
Buckwheat Pancake mix
½ pint sour cream, cold
4 tbsps. hot melted butter
6 tbsps. caviar

The How
Mix a thin batter with the pancake mix and make a dozen thin pancakes about 4 inches in diameter. Pour a little melted butter in each cake as you stack them on a warm plate. Put a tablespoon of sour cream in the center of each pancake, then a tablespoon of caviar on the cream. Fold pancake over filling and serve—two to a person.

Crabes au Riz
Crabmeat with rice.

The What
1 cup cooked rice
1 cup mayonnaise
1 tbsp. lemon juice
1 tbsp. parsley flakes

1 lb. crabmeat, or lobster
3 tbsps. capers
paprika

The How
Mix mayonnaise, lemon juice, parsley, and half the capers. Mix half the mayonnaise mixture with the cooled rice and form into a bed on chilled serving dish. Mix remaining mayonnaise mixture with crabmeat and mound on rice. Sprinkle with balance of capers and paprika for extra color.

Cornets de Jambon
Stuffed ham cones.

The What
1 cup frozen cooked mixed vegetables
½ tbsp. plain gelatin
1 10-oz. can consommé
6 slices boiled ham
6 conical paper cups

The How
Drain vegetables well in sieve or colander. Dissolve gelatin in consommé and mix with vegetables. Fit a slice of ham in each cup, trimming so it fits exactly. Chill vegetable mixture until thickened. Press into cups and refrigerate until set. Unmold and pipe on mayonnaise. Put in wheel spoke designing on serving platter before piping with mayonnaise. NOTE: An extra paper cup with the point cut off makes a one-shot piping bag.

Homard en Croute
Lobster turnovers.

The What
1 package buttermilk biscuits
1 5½-oz. can lobster meat
green butter (see sauces)

The How
Roll out biscuits until about ¼ inch thick. Put a tablespoon lobster meat and 1 teaspoon green butter in center of each biscuit. Brush edges with water and fold over, pressing edges firmly to seal. Bake according to package directions.

Fondue Suisse
Swiss cheese fondue.

1 pkg. refrigerated swiss fondue
3 button mushrooms, sliced thin
1 oz. Kirsch liqueur
1 small loaf French bread

The How
Heat cheese according to package directions. Add Kirsch and mushrooms. Cut the bread in 2" cubes. Serve fondue in small casseroles or dipping dishes. Spear bread with fork and dip into cheese. NOTE: If you have a chafing dish be clubby and serve the fondue that way, giving each guest a long fork.

SOUPS

Soupe à l'Oignon
Onion soup.

Suddenly French

The What
1 can condensed onion soup (10½ ozs.)
¾ soup can water
6 tbsps. grated Swiss cheese
3 tbsps. grated Parmesan cheese
3 tbsps. butter
3 slices French bread, toasted

The How
Heat and mix soup and water and divide evenly into 3 small casseroles. Put 2 tablespoons Swiss cheese and 1 tablespoon butter in each. Put in slices of toast and sprinkle on Parmesan cheese. Heat at 350° until cheese is melted. *Serves 3.*

Consommé aux Champignons
Beef broth and mushrooms

The What
6 white medium mushrooms
3 tbsps. lemon juice
2 cups beef broth
1 tsp. parsley flakes, or chive flakes

The How
Slice mushrooms thin and toss in lemon juice. After 5 minutes drain and add to heated broth. Heat just under boiling 5 minutes. Sprinkle with parsley. *Serves 3.*

Consommé Bellevue
Clam and chicken broth.

The What
2 tbsps chopped chives

1 can clam juice
1 can chicken bouillon
4 ozs. sour cream
1 tbsp. parsley flakes

The How
Heat clam juice, bouillon, and parsley. Top with sour cream and chopped chives in each serving, or serve on the side if you are not sure how your guests feel about sour cream.

Potage Duchesse
Cream of cauliflower soup.

The What
1 pkg. (10 ozs.) frozen cauliflower, cooked
1 10-oz. can cream of potato soup
1½ soup cans milk
3 tbsps. butter
1 tbsp. chopped chives
1 tsp. dry mustard
croutons

The How
Mix and heat all ingredients except chives and croutons. Mash cauliflower thoroughly, or blend in blender. Add chives and serve with bowl of croutons.

Creme d'Epinard
Cream of spinach soup.

The What
14 ozs. chicken broth

1 4-oz. jar chopped spinach (baby food)
¼ tsp. thyme
2 tbsps. sherry

The How
Heat soup and spinach, but do not boil. Add thyme and sherry. Let stand 5 minutes, then serve with hot croutons.

Potage Cingalaise
Curried chicken cream soup.

The What
1 10½-oz. can condensed cream of chicken soup
1 soup can milk
1 tsp. curry powder
1 tsp. lemon juice

The How
Warm soup and add other ingredients. Do not boil. Serve hot or cold with hot croutons or finger rolls.

Bisque de Crevettes et Homard
Shrimp and lobster soup.

The What
2 or 3 ozs. lobster meat, shredded
1 can (10 ozs.) frozen cream of shrimp soup
⅛ tsp. paprika
⅛ tsp. basil
1 tbsp. butter
1 soup can whole milk
salt and pepper to taste

The How
Mix all ingredients and heat, but do not boil. Float croutons or oyster crackers on top, or serve on side. *Serves 2 generously.*

MEAT DISHES

Langue de Boeuf au Gratin
Beef tongue, ham, and cheese.

The What
1½ lbs. canned beef tongue
½ lb. sliced boiled ham
¾ cup canned gravy
½ cup white wine
1 can (3 or 4 ozs.) chopped mushrooms
½ cup bread crumbs
½ cup cheddar cheese (grated)
4 tbsps. butter
1 tbsp. parsley flakes
1 tbsp. tomato paste

The How
Heat wine, half of the parsley, mushrooms, tomato paste, and half the butter together. Mix cheese, balance of parsley, and bread crumbs. Slice tongue and alternate slices of tongue and ham in a shallow baking dish. Pour sauce over meat and sprinkle cheese-crumb mixture on top. Dot with remaining butter. Brown lightly under moderate broiler heat. *Serves 6 or 8.*

Foie de Veau à l'Orange
Calves liver in orange sauce.

The What
8 thin slices calves liver
½ cup flour
1 tsp. salt
½ tsp. dry mustard
½ tsp. pepper
4 tbsps. butter
¼ tsp. tarragon
1 tbsp. instant onion or flakes
¼ tsp. garlic powder
¼ cup beef broth
¼ cup Burgundy or other red wine
1 can (10 ozs.) Mandarin orange sections, drained

The How
Shake liver in paper bag with flour and seasonings and sauté it in half the butter until golden. Remove to warm platter. Add balance of ingredients, except oranges, and stir-cook, being sure to scrape brown glaze from bottom of pan into sauce. Add oranges and stir until heated. Pour sauce over liver and serve.

Ris de Veau Marsala
This dish, sweetbreads in Marsala wine, requires partial preparation one day before serving.

The What
2 veal sweetbreads
½ cup Marsala wine
1 tbsp. instant onion
1 tsp. parsley flakes
¼ tsp. thyme
3 tbsps. butter

The How
Wash sweetbreads, place in saucepan, and cover with cold water, adding 1 tsp. salt. Boil and then simmer 7 minutes. Drain well. Put sweetbreads on a plate and weight with another plate until cool. Peel off thin skin and trim off any tendons. Slice in two crosswise and refrigerate overnight. To prepare, brown in butter in frying pan, adding onion when half finished. Remove meat to platter. Add seasonings to butter, then the wine. Stir-cook 3 minutes. Pour sauce over meat and serve.

Boeuf Braise
Braised beef in onion soup.

The What
3½ lbs. bottom round of beef
3 tbsps. bacon fat
3 tbsps. flour
1 tsp. salt
1 pkg. dehydrated onion soup mix
½ cup hot water
½ cup dry red wine
¼ tsp. pepper

The How
Mix flour and salt and rub into roast. Melt fat in Dutch oven or heavy pot and sear roast all around until lightly browned. Add all other ingredients. Bring to a boil. Cover tightly and simmer 3 hours. Fifteen minutes before roast is done, you may want to add a can of small peeled potatoes. *Serves 4 to 6.*

Cotelettes d'Agneau
Lamb chops in tomato sauce.

The What
4 lamb chops
1 can (8 ozs.) tomato sauce
¼ tsp. garlic powder
1 egg beaten with 1 tsp. milk
¼ tsp. oregano
½ cup fine dry bread crumbs
2 tbsps. olive oil (or other cooking oil)
¼ tsp. pepper, ½ tsp. salt

The How
Wipe chops with a slightly damp cloth. Mix salt, pepper, oregano, garlic, and crumbs. Dip chops in egg, then in crumbs. Fry chops brown on each side in oil. Pour tomato sauce over. Cover and heat 5 minutes. *Serves 2.*

Boeuf à la Mode
You spend 20 minutes. The oven does the work for braised beef in red wine.

The What
4½ lbs. beef rump
1 can (10½ ozs.) consommé
2 cups red wine
4 strips bacon
1 can diced carrots
2 tbsps. bacon fat
1 can small whole onions
3 tbsps. flour
1 bay leaf
1 cup canned beef gravy

The How
Put roast in a bowl and pour wine over. Let stand in wine

for 5 to 6 hours, turning 3 or 4 times during the marinating time. Dry off thoroughly and dust with flour. Brown all around in the fat. Remove and add 1½ cups of the marinade and the bay leaf to pot. Bring to boil and stir in consommé and gravy. Return meat to pot. Put bacon strips on top. Cover and bake at 350° 3½ hours. Put in vegetables, cover, and heat 10 more minutes. *Serves 6 to 8.*

Pot au Feu
Chicken and beef in the pot.

The What
1 lb. diced stewing beef
4 chicken legs
2 cups chicken broth
1½ cups beef broth
4 tbsps. butter or oil
1 can (12 ozs.) small carrots
1 cup chopped celery, or 3 tbsps. celery flakes
1 tbsp. parsley flakes
1 tbsp. flour *mixed with:*
1 tbsp. butter
3 tbsps. white wine

The How
Season beef with salt and pepper and brown in butter. Remove and brown chicken. Return beef to pot. Add beef and chicken broth, celery, and parsley flakes. Simmer one half hour, covered. Remove chicken. Cook beef one hour. Add flour and butter mixture and stir well. Add chicken and carrots and heat. *Serves 4.*

Boeuf Bourguignon
Braised beef with burgundy.

The What
1½ lbs. round steak, in one-half-inch cubes
2 cups canned gravy
1 cup Burgundy
½ cup canned sliced mushrooms
1 can small whole onions
½ tsp. each: salt, pepper, thyme
1 tbsp. parsley flakes

The How
Heat oil in heavy pot or flameproof casserole. Brown meat cubes and sprinkle with seasonings. Add gravy, juice from mushrooms, and wine. Cover and simmer 1 hour. Add mushrooms and onions and sprinkle with parsley. Heat and serve to 4.

Tournedos Bearnaise
Broiled filet in Bearnaise sauce.

The What
4 one-inch-thick beef filet slices
1 tsp. parsley flakes
1 tsp. chive flakes
½ tsp. tarragon
4 tbsps. butter
8 ozs. Bearnaise sauce

The How
Broil steaks. Heat Bearnaise with herbs in a double boiler.

Put steaks on a hot platter, and top each with 1 tbsp. butter. Spoon on a little Bearnaise, and serve balance in a gravy dish. *Serves 4.* NOTE: Pork chops or loin chops are also delicious served this way.

Escalopes de Veau aux Champignons
Veal and mushrooms.

The What
8 scallops of veal
2 tbsps. onion flakes or instant minced
1 3-oz. can sliced mushrooms
½ cup Sauterne or other white table wine
½ cup heavy cream
½ cup beef broth or consommé
1 tbsp. parsley flakes
4 tbsps. butter

The How
If you know an Italian butcher he will cut and pound the veal scallops thin. Otherwise use a steak pounder. Heat half the butter and brown scallops, 3 minutes on one side and 2 minutes on the other. Remove from pan and add balance of butter. Cook onions 2 minutes then add mushrooms, wine, and broth. Stir in cream and stir-cook until slightly thickened. Add parsley and scallops and heat. *Serves 4.*

SEA FOODS

Homard à l'Armoricaine
Lobster in tomato-brandy sauce.

Suddenly French

The What
6 frozen lobster tails
6 tbsps. butter or margarine
3 tbsps. instant minced onion
1 cup white wine
2 cups beef broth or bouillon
¼ cup brandy
1 cup drained canned tomatoes
¼ tsp. thyme
2 tbsps. flour mixed with 1 tbsp. butter
2 tsps. tomato paste
salt and pepper

The How
Thaw and split lobster tails. Sauté, meat side down, in butter 8 minutes. Turn and cook 5 minutes. Add onions and sauté 2 minutes. Add brandy and ignite. (Stand away when lighting.) Add balance of ingredients except tomatoes and flour-butter mixture. Cover and simmer 20 minutes. Stir in flour-butter mixture and stir-cook until thickened. Add tomatoes and heat. Season to taste.

Filet de Sole, Amandine
Sole with slivered almonds.

The What
1 package frozen cooked fillets of sole
¼ lb. butter
½ cup blanched slivered almonds
½ tsp. sweet basil
2 tbsps. sherry

The How
Heat fish in butter and remove to heated oven dish.

Brown almonds in butter. Sprinkle in basil and add sherry. Pour over fillets. Keep hot and serve when ready.

Bouillabaisse
In spite of all the glamor attached to the name, bouillabaisse is just a succulent fish stew that can be quick and simple, yet as tasty as the gourmet recipes that take hours to prepare. With the help of the frozen food counter and the cans from the market shelves, it's a breeze. Of course, if you live on the coast, you can use clam and lobster in the shell, for a more colorful dish!

The What
1 frozen lobster tail
10 clams, in shell, canned
1 5-oz. can lobster meat
1 small sea bass, or other fresh fish, cleaned and cut in half
2 tbsps. butter
1 tbsp. instant onion
1 cup canned tomatoes
½ cup clam juice
¼ tsp. saffron
¼ tsp. garlic powder
¼ tsp. black pepper
½ cup white wine
1 tsp. parsley flakes
1 tsp. chive flakes

The How
Sauté onions two minutes in butter. Stir in parsley and seasonings. Add tomatoes, wine and clam juice and simmer 3 minutes. Add fish and cook covered 8 minutes,

together with halved lobster tail. Add clams and lobster meat and heat. Serve over a slice of toasted French bread and sprinkle with chives.

Truite au Bleu en Gelée
Blue trout in aspic.

The What
2 frozen rainbow trout, thawed
1 small can pimentos
2 tbsps. wine vinegar
3 cups clam juice
1 envelope plain gelatin
1 bunch watercress
½ cup sliced mushrooms, fried in butter (available in cans)

The How
Bring clam juice and vinegar to a boil in a pot just large enough to lay the trout in. Put in fish. Cover, and simmer 8 minutes. Remove and peel off skin, leaving head and tail intact. Put on a platter to cool. Soften gelatin in ¼ cup cold water, then add to 1½ cups of the broth you cooked the fish in. Let cool until as thick as raw egg white. Brush on fish, turning until coated. Pour balance of gelatin on plate and refrigerate. Before it hardens, dip strips of pimento and mushrooms into gelatin and decorate trout with them. Chop hard gelatin and surround the fish with it. Garnish with watercress.

Huîtres en Epinard
This is a version of Oysters Rockefeller.

The What
1 doz. large oysters
4 tbsps. butter
2 tbsps. sour cream
1 pkg. (12 ozs.) frozen chopped spinach

The How
Cook spinach in juice from oysters until just barely tender. Drain and season. Stir in half the butter and all the sour cream. Divide among 3 or 4 shallow casseroles. Place oysters on top of spinach and press down gently. Season with coarse black pepper and place under moderate broiler until edges of oysters curl. Remove and serve over toast points or with croutons. *Serves 2 to 4.*

Truite au Beurre
Trout in butter sauce.

The What
2 frozen rainbow trout
2 tbsps. butter
1 tbsp. lemon juice
1 tbsp. chive flakes

The How
Defrost trout completely. Place on rack in roasting pan, adding about ½ inch of water. Water must not touch fish. Cover and steam until tender, about 20 minutes. Slide fish off rack onto platter. Lemon juice, combined with chives and melted butter, is poured over fish.

Grenouilles à la Provençale
Frog's legs gourmet.

The What
4 tbsps. butter
6 pair frozen frog's legs
1 egg, beaten
½ cup fine crumbs, cracker or bread
2 tbsps. tomato paste
½ tsp. garlic powder
1 tbsp. lemon juice
2 tbsps. white wine
½ cup tomato juice
¼ tsp. black pepper
½ tsp. salt
1 tbsp. flour

The How
Thaw frog's legs completely. Dip first in beaten egg and then in crumbs, and fry in butter until lightly browned all over. Remove from pan. Mix flour, garlic powder and lemon juice well. Put balance of ingredients into pan and stir-cook until thickened. Add frog's legs and heat. *Serves 2 to 3.*

Crevettes au Curry
Shrimp in curry sauce.

The What
2 pkgs. (12 ozs. each) frozen peeled shrimp
1½ tsps. curry powder
1 tbsp. lemon juice
1 tbsp. parsley flakes
1 can (10 ozs.) condensed cream of chicken soup

The How
Cook shrimp 5 minutes in boiling water and then drain.

Heat soup with lemon juice, curry powder, and parsley. Add shrimp and reheat. Serve with instant rice and chutney. *Serves 6.*

Scampi Moderne
Broiled shrimp.

The What
2 lbs. large fresh shrimp in shell
8 tbsps. melted butter
1 tsp. garlic powder
1 tsp. salt

The How
Arrange shrimp in single layer on flat baking sheet, first dipping in butter. Dust with salt and garlic powder, and broil until shells turn pink. Turn once and broil so both sides are pink, dusting again with seasoning after turning. *Serves 6.*

VEGETABLES

With the French, vegetables are not automatically served with the main course, or on the same plate. For instance, asparagus with Hollandaise may be a first course. You may find meat or fish served only with a garnish, such as sprigs of parsley or watercress. Remember, a sauce is an accent, not a cover, so never use too much. Colorful garnishes are part of the appeal of the French cuisine, so garnish for eye appeal, as well as for taste.

Petit Pois Robert
A switch on green peas.

The What
1 pkg. frozen small green peas
¼ cup coarsely diced ham
3 tbsps. butter
¼ tsp. parsley flakes or chervil flakes
⅔ cup canned chicken broth
8 scallions and two lettuce leaves

The How
Wash scallions and discard green tops and roots. Chop lettuce leaves about 1 inch square. Put all ingredients in saucepan, except peas and lettuce. Cook until scallions are tender. Sprinkle with coarse black pepper, add frozen peas and lettuce, and simmer 3 minutes. *Serves 4.*

Epinard à la Crème
Spinach in sour cream sauce.

The What
1 pkg. frozen chopped spinach
1 tbsp. butter
2 tbsps. sour cream
¼ tsp. black pepper

The How
Cook spinach and drain well. Do not overcook. Return to pan with butter and pepper. Toss with butter and remove from heat. Add sour cream and serve. *Serves 2 or 3.*

Riz Vert
Green rice.

The What
instant rice, prepared to make 1 cup

3 tbsps. butter
5 tbsps. chopped cooked (canned) spinach
½ tsp. sage

The How
Stir all ingredients into hot rice and serve at once. Serves 2.

Champignons au Sherry
Mushrooms in sherry sauce.

The What
1 lb. fresh mushrooms
3 tbsps. butter
3 ozs. sherry
⅛ tsp. thyme

The How
Slice mushrooms and fry in butter for 3 minutes. Sprinkle with thyme and pour sherry over. Stir-cook 2 minutes. Serves 4.

Asperge Vinaigrette
Asparagus in vinaigrette sauce.

The What
2 pkgs. asparagus tips, frozen
1 hard-boiled egg
1 jar (2 ozs.) pimento
8 black olives

The How
Cook asparagus as directed on package. Drain and chill.

Suddenly French

Chop egg, pimento, and olives and mix. Moisten with Italian dressing and serve over asparagus. *Serves 4 to 6.*

Pommes de Terre au Caviar
Potatoes with caviar.

The What
2 large baked Idaho potatoes
2 tbsps. caviar
2 tbsps. sour cream

The How
Gash each potato and open slightly. Put a tablespoon of sour cream in each, then a tablespoon of caviar. *Serves 2.* This is excellent with a light meat course such as Côtelettes à la Kiev.

Artichauts Maitre d'Hotel
Artichoke hearts, dressed.

The What
1 pkg. frozen artichoke hearts
1 tsp. lemon juice
2 tbsps. butter
1 tsp. parsley flakes
1 tbsp. chive flakes

The How
Cook artichokes and drain. Return to pan with balance of ingredients and shake over heat until butter is melted. Toss to blend well. *Serves 3.*

FOWL

Caneton à l'Orange
Duckling with orange sauce.

The What
1 duckling (4 to 6 lbs.)
1 tsp. salt
½ tsp. garlic powder
1 orange, peeled and sectioned
¾ cup beef gravy, canned
1 cup Burgundy or other red wine
2 tbsps. currant jelly
2 tbsps. grated orange peel
3 tbsps. Cointreau
1 can Mandarin orange sections
1 tsp. thyme

The How
Mix thyme, salt, and garlic powder and rub duck inside and out. Roast, breast up 25 minutes per pound in 350° oven. Baste with orange juice twice during cooking. When done, remove to warm platter. Add balance of ingredients to pan (except Mandarin sections) and boil 5 minutes. Add Mandarin sections and heat. Pour sauce over duck and serve 4 or 5.

Coq au Vin
Chicken de Luxe.

The What
1 frying chicken (3 lbs., cut up)
½ tsp. garlic powder

4 tbsps. butter
2 cups red wine
⅓ cup brandy
¼ tsp. thyme
¼ tsp. chervil
1 tbsp. butter, mixed with 1 tbsp. flour
1 can small white onions
3 ozs. mushrooms, fried slowly in butter

The How
Brown chicken pieces in skillet with butter and garlic powder. When done, pour brandy over chicken and ignite. When flame dies add wine and herbs. Cover and cook slowly 25 minutes until chicken is done. Stir in flour-butter mixture and stir-cook until thickened. Add onions and mushrooms and heat. Transfer all to heated casserole and serve to 4 to 6. If you have individual ramekins you will be going first class in the finest French tradition.

Poulet Sauté à la Marengo
Chicken with lobster.

The What
3 lbs. cut up frying chicken
2 rock lobster tails
2 tbsps. tomato paste
½ tsp. chervil
2 tbsps. parsley flakes
4 tbsps. butter
4 eggs
1 cup canned mushroom gravy
½ cup white wine
1 cup garlic-flavored croutons
salt and pepper

The How
Brown chicken in butter in large skillet. Season with salt and pepper. Add rock lobster, tomato paste, chervil, gravy, half the parsley, and wine. Cover and cook 25 minutes. Add croutons, heat, and turn onto hot serving platter. Top with 4 fried eggs and sprinkle with parsley. *Serves 4 to 5.* We are not sure what the fried eggs are added for. Maybe the French know, as this is how they insist Chicken Marengo should be served.

Suprêmes de Volaille
Supreme breasts of chicken.

The What
meat from 3 chicken breasts, pounded thin
2 tsps. dried grated lemon rind
2 tbsps. bottled lemon juice
1 cup cream
6 pats butter
¼ lb. butter
2 tbsps. sherry
salt and pepper
2 tbsps. grated Parmesan cheese
¼ tsp. savory

The How
Season chicken breasts and sauté 4 minutes on each side in butter. Remove to shallow baking dish. Put in balance of ingredients except Parmesan and butter pats in skillet and stir-cook until slightly thickened. Pour over chicken, put a pat of butter on each piece and sprinkle with the cheese. Brown lightly under broiler and serve. *Serves 4 or 5.*

Suprêmes Milanese
Chicken breasts Italian style.

The What
2 chicken breasts, boned and pounded thin
¼ lb. butter
¼ tsp. rosemary
4 slices lemon
1 cup flour
½ cup fine bread crumbs
1 egg
1 tbsp. milk
½ tsp. salt
¼ tsp. pepper
½ cup grated Parmesan cheese

The How
Put flour and seasonings in paper bag. Beat egg with milk. Mix cheese and bread crumbs. Put chicken pieces into bag and shake until coated with flour. Dip into egg wash and roll in crumb-cheese mixture. Sauté brown in hot butter (foaming hot) in skillet, 4 minutes on each side. Serve, decorating each piece with a lemon slice.

Poulet à l'Estragon
Tarragon chicken breasts.

The What
3 chicken breasts, boned, skinned, and halved
1 can (6 or 8 ozs.) chicken pâté
1 can condensed chicken broth
1 can chicken gravy
1 tsp. tarragon flakes
6 sprigs parsley

The How
Put chicken in saucepan with ⅔ teaspoon tarragon and the chicken broth. Cover and cook until tender, about 20 minutes. Remove and cut a pocket in each piece and stuff with 1 tablespoon of chicken pâté. Heat gravy in another pan with balance of tarragon. Add chicken pieces and reheat just until hot. *Serves 6.*

Côtelettes à la Kiev
Chicken cutlets Russian style.

The What
2 chicken breasts, boned and beaten thin
4 tbsps. green butter (see sauces)
1 cup flour
1 egg, lightly beaten
1 cup vegetable oil
1 cup fine bread crumbs
salt and pepper
¼ tsp. thyme

The How
Sprinkle salt, pepper, and thyme on each chicken piece and rub in. Put 1 tablespoon cold green butter on each piece and fold in sides. Then fold ends over and fasten with toothpicks. Dip into flour, then into egg, then coat with bread crumbs. Deep fry in oil (should be 375°) for 5 minutes. Drain and remove picks. *Serves 4.*

SAUCES

Some people believe sauce is the core of French cuisine.

Some like the taste of the food au naturel. The secret is to use just a little sauce for appearance and serve the rest on the side for true sauce lovers.

Mayonnaise Vert
Green mayonnaise.

The What
1 cup mayonnaise
1 tbsp. parsley flakes
1 tbsp. dill flakes
2 tbsps. chive flakes
1 tbsp. lemon juice

The How
Mix all ingredients well and let stand overnight to develop flavor.

Beurre Vert
Green butter.

The What

½ cup sweet butter, softened
2 tbsps. chives, chopped, or flakes
¼ tsp. lemon juice
1 tbsp. parsley flakes

The How
Mix all ingredients well. Keep refrigerated. Excellent with steaks, chops, or as called for in recipes.

Sauce Brune
Instant brown sauce.

The What
1 can beef gravy (10 ozs.)
4 ozs. Burgundy or other red wine
⅛ tsp. celery powder

The How
Heat gravy to boiling. Reduce heat and stir in wine and seasonings. If thinner sauce is desired, add more wine. Serve with almost any cooked meat.

Sauce Champignons
Mushroom sauce.

The What
1 can (10 ozs.) beef gravy
3 ozs. Madeira wine
1 4-oz. can mushrooms
juice from mushrooms
1 tbsp. butter
1 tsp. parsley flakes

The How
Heat gravy and add wine, mushroom juice, parsley, sliced mushrooms, and butter. Serve with steaks, rolled roasts, or meat pies.

Beurre de Crevettes
Shrimp butter.

The What
½ cup cooked or canned shrimp
¼ lb. melted butter
1 tbsp. tomato paste
½ tbsp. tarragon flakes

The How
Put ingredients in blender, and leave ½ minute on medium speed. Keep refrigerated. Serve on canapés or as a garnish on hot or cold fish dishes.

Beurre de Manie
Butter and flour roux.

Butter and flour mixed smoothly, half and half. Keeps well when refrigerated. Used for thickening pan gravy, sauces. Stir into hot sauces or gravies and stir-cook about 3 minutes.

Sauce au Madère
Madeira wine sauce.

The What
1 can (10 ozs.) beef gravy
1½ tbsps. butter
4 ozs. Madeira wine
1 pinch cayenne pepper

The How
Heat gravy with butter, then stir in wine and pepper. Keeps well when refrigerated. Use on beef, veal, meatloaf, lamb.

Sauce à la Provençale
Tomato, garlic, and herb sauce.

The What
1 can (8 ozs.) tomato sauce
½ tsp. garlic powder
½ tbsp. parsley flakes

½ tbsp. chive flakes
1 tsp. grated orange peel
¼ tsp. saffron (optional)

The How
Heat all ingredients together but do not boil. Let stand at least a half hour for flavors to blend. Reheat and serve on meats, spaghetti, or pastas.

Sauce au Curry
Curry sauce.

The What
1 can condensed cream of chicken soup
½ can light cream
1 tsp. curry powder

The How
Heat all ingredients together. Serve over cooked meats, poultry, vegetables, or fish.

Sauce Mornay
Instant mornay sauce.

The What
1 can cheese soup
½ can light cream
½ tsp. paprika
¼ tsp. white pepper

The How
Heat everything together but do not boil. Serve over broccoli or other vegetables with turkey or fish. Brown

lightly under broiler. Do not blacken the top, as cheese and cream will darken very quickly.

DESSERTS

The smart host or hostess knows that a heavy dessert after a hearty meal detracts from the total effect and makes your overfed guests dull company. Keep your desserts light both in content and portion, and your guests will love you. The calorie counters will give you high marks as a smart hostess.

Croquembouche au Caramel
Caramel iced cream puffs.

The What
1 doz. cream puffs, custard filled
1 cup lump sugar
½ cup water
1 tbsp. corn syrup

The How
Combine syrup, sugar, and water in saucepan. Cook at medium heat until sugar melts. Turn up heat and cook until light brown color. Put cream puffs in aluminum foil. Cool caramel to about 100° and then pour on each puff. Let cool until caramel is set and keep cool until serving. *Serves 6.*

Crêpes Suzettes Jubilee
Thin pancakes with cherries.

The What
1 cup pitted black cherries, drained
4 tbsps. red currant jelly
4 tbsps. orange marmalade
2 tbsps. cherry juice
2 tbsps. brandy
2 pkgs. (6 each) frozen cherry blintzes

The How
Heat blintzes as directed on package. Heat the 2 tablespoons cherry juice and stir in marmalade and jelly. Stir until melted. Add brandy and cherries. Warm and pour over blintzes. Serve hot to 6.

Brioches au Chocolat
Brioche is a small semi-sweet roll, topped with chocolate, that is light, easy to prepare, and very tasty.

The What
4 brioches
4 ozs. chocolate sauce
4 small mint icing candies

The How
Slice top knob off each brioche. Pour sauce on open part of brioche and top with mint. Serve warm. *Serves 4.*

Petit Pots de Crême au Café
Coffee and caramel pudding.

The What
1 pkg. vanilla pudding
3/4 cup milk

Suddenly French

¾ cup light cream
1 egg yolk
1 tbsp. corn syrup
4 tbsps. instant coffee
½ cup water
1 cup sugar

The How

Heat water, sugar, and corn syrup in skillet without stirring until sugar melts. Turn up heat and cook until dark brown. Pour 2 tablespoons of this sauce in each of 4 custard cups. Move cup around so caramel coats well all around inside. Prepare pudding as directed on package, using the milk and cream instead of 2 cups milk as directed. Bring to full boil. Turn down heat. Add lightly beaten egg yolk and coffee while stirring and cooking. Pour into custard cups and chill. Top with salted almonds. *Serves 4.*

Bombe Boule de Neiges
Fruit and ice cream snowball.

The What
⅔ cup mixed chopped candied fruits
½ cup kirsch
1 cup whipping cream, whipped
2 doz. crystallized violets
3 pts. vanilla ice cream

The How
Soften ice cream a little. Blend with fruit, which has been soaked in Kirsch for 1 hour. Pack into a 2-quart round mold. Freeze until ice cream hardens. Unmold onto a

chilled round platter. Decorate with whipped cream and top with violets.

Pêches au Champagne
Peaches in champagne.

The What
6 peach halves, marinated in 4 tbsps. brandy
6 large strawberries

The How
Put ½ peach in a champagne glass. In the pit cavity, place strawberry. Drizzle a little peach syrup-brandy mixture over top. Repeat until 6 servings are prepared.

Pêches au Vin Rouge
Peaches in red wine.

The What
6 large peaches, unpeeled and washed
¾ cup sugar
1 tbsp. orange marmalade
1 cup medium dry red wine
1 cup water
6 halves maraschino cherries

The How
Bring sugar, marmalade, wine, and water to a boil. Add peaches. Cook until peaches are just tender. Serve topped with a half maraschino cherry. *Serves 6.*

Coupe au Marrons
Ice cream and chestnuts.

The What
1 can chestnuts in vanilla syrup
1 pint vanilla ice cream
1 cup whipped cream

The How
Chop chestnuts coarsely and return to syrup. Spoon chestnuts on top of each serving of ice cream and top with whipped cream.

Gelée de Café Irlandais
Jellied Irish coffee.

The What
¼ cup Irish whiskey
1½ tbsps. instant coffee
6 tbsps. whipped cream
1 envelope (1 tbsp.) plain gelatin
¼ cup sugar
1½ cups hot water
12 water ice wafers

The How
Soften gelatin in ½ cup cold water. Heat 1 cup water in saucepan. Dissolve coffee and add gelatin and sugar. Cool and add whiskey. Put in demi-tasse cups and chill until set. Serve with topping of whipped cream and 2 water ice wafers. *Serves 6.*

8. Party Cooking with Wine

Through the years, gourmet chefs have used wine to add distinctive flavor to food. The knowledgeable use of wine in cookery enhances taste and improves digestibility. Here are many uses of wine in food preparation. The possibilities are endless, governed only by your taste and imagination.

Party Steak Pot
The What
2 lbs. tender beefsteak, cut 1" thick
¼ cup butter
1½ tsps. seasoned salt (or celery salt)
⅔ cup Chablis or Sauterne
¼ cup ketchup
2 tsps. cornstarch
¼ tsp. dill flakes
freshly ground black pepper

The How
Trim fat off steak and cut into bite-size cubes, about ½" thick. Brown steak quickly in butter, turning and sprin-

kling with salt and pepper. Steak will be medium rare at this point. Remove steak to heated chafing dish. Blend wine, ketchup, cornstarch, dill, and pepper to taste. Stir into pan drippings. Cook and stir until mixture boils and thickens. Pour over steak cubes, stirring to coat and combine. Serve with fondue forks or long cocktail picks, with dishes of dip-alongs (chopped chives mixed with chopped parsley, toasted sesame seeds, ground toasted almonds, mixture of mustard and chili-sauce, or sour cream mixed with chopped chutney) on the side.

Sherried Green Pea Soup
The What
1 can split green pea soup
1 soup can of milk
1 7-oz. can minced clams, undrained
½ cup medium sherry

The How
Mix soup, milk, clams, and juice in saucepan. Bring to bubble, then remove from heat. Just before serving add sherry. Garnish with chive flakes or garlic croutons, if you desire. *Serves 4.*

TO MAKE GARLIC CROUTONS, blend garlic powder into soft butter (½ tsp. powder to ½ lb. butter). Butter bread both sides. Cut into cubes and toast lightly under broiler.

Golden Cheese Soup
The What
1 can cheddar cheese soup
1 cup coffee cream
½ cup dairy sour cream

1 tsp. parsley flakes
⅛ tsp. celery seed
¼ cup dry sherry

The How
Heat soup and cream together. When beginning to bubble nicely, remove from heat and stir in sherry. Mix sour cream, parsley, and celery seed, and drop a spoonful on each serving or serve on the side. *Serves 4 or 5.*

Wine Party Spread
The What
1⅓ cups cheddar cheese spread
1 tsp. grated orange rind
1 cup cream cottage cheese
½ tsp. tarragon flakes
¼ cup dry vermouth

The How
Beat cheese spread with vermouth until smooth. Beat in orange rind, tarragon, and cottage cheese. *Makes about 2 cups.*

Baked Fish Fillets Tartare
The What
2 cups Sauterne
2 tbsps. salt
2 lbs. fish fillets, fresh or frozen
1 cup dry bread crumbs
2 tbsps. onion flakes
1 cup dairy sour cream
½ cup mayonnaise
½ cup light cream
paprika

The How
Marinate fish in wine and salt for 3 hours, turning, unless fillets are covered with marinade. Drain well on paper towels. Dip in bread crumbs. Put in shallow baking dish. Spread mixture of mayonnaise, onion and sour cream, over fillets. Cover with thin layer of crumbs and dust with paprika. Bake in preheated 500° oven 12 to 15 minutes, depending on whether fillets are thick or thin. *Serves 6.*

Consommé Ham-Rice
The What
3 tbsps. butter
1 pkg. (5 ozs.) quick-cooking rice
1 can (10½ ozs.) condensed consommé
1 (2 ozs.) can undrained mushrooms
4 tbsps. instant onion
1 cup cooked ham, chopped fine
½ cup Sauterne or Chablis

The How
Melt butter in saucepan. Add rice and stir-cook until rice is golden. Add balance of ingredients and bring to boil. Cover and simmer for 5 minutes. Remove from direct heat, but keep warm for 15 minutes before serving. Fluff gently before serving. *Serves 4.*

Sherried Cheeseburgers
The What
1 pkg. cheese sauce mix
½ cup milk
½ cup sherry (medium)
3 tbsps. bacon drippings
½ lb. ground beef

½ lb. ground pork
1 tsp. salt
¼ tsp. black pepper
1 tbsp. onion flakes
4 hamburger buns
4 slices tomato

The How
Mix cheese sauce, milk, and wine, and heat to boil, stirring steadily. Hold hot over hot water. Mix beef, pork, onion, and seasonings and shape into 4 patties. Sauté in bacon fat until browned and cooked. Place meat patty on ½ hamburger bun on plates. Top with tomato slice, and pour on sauce. Serve other half of bun on side, with pickle relish.

Burgunchilis
The What
½ tsp. salt
½ tsp. pepper
1 tbsp. onion flakes
¾ lb. ground beef
¼ lb. ground pork
2 cans (15 ozs. each) chili con carne with beans
3 tbsps. bacon fat drippings
½ cup Burgundy
½ cup bread crumbs
4 hamburger buns

The How
Mix onion, seasonings, and meat. Shape into 4 patties to fit buns. Brown well on both sides in fat. Heat chili, wine,

and crumbs. Pour over patties and simmer five minutes. Put 2 bun halves on each plate. Put meat patty on one half and pour sauce on top. Heap chili beans on other half. *Serves 4.*

Chicken Curry All-of-a-Sudden
The What
2 cans (5 ozs. each) chicken
1 can (10½ ozs.) cream of chicken soup
1 tsp. curry powder
1 tsp. butter
¼ cup Sauterne
3 cups cooked rice

The How
Melt butter and mix in curry. Add balance of ingredients, except rice, and heat slowly until hot. Serve over hot rice. For a gourmet touch serve as topping or on the side: chutney, pineapple chunks, chopped peanuts, or crumbled crisp bacon. *Serves 4.*

Scampi Chablis
The What
2 cans (5 ozs.) drained shrimp
4 tbsps. butter
2 tbsps. parsley flakes
⅛ tsp. garlic powder or chips
½ cup Chablis

The How
Melt butter in chafing dish or skillet. Add shrimp, garlic, parsley, and wine. Heat to slow simmer. Serve over toast or from chafing dish. *Serves 4.*

Casserole Epicure
The What
2 tbsps. bacon fat
2 lbs. stewing beef in 1-inch chunks
2 cans (10½ ozs. each) condensed consommé
½ tsp. salt
½ tsp. oregano flakes
4 tbsps. instant onion flakes
½ cup flour
½ cup fine bread crumbs
1 cup Burgundy or Claret

The How
Roll beef in flour and brown in fat. Mix remaining flour with bread crumbs, then with consommé. Put beef and balance of ingredients in casserole. Bake covered 3 hours at 300°. *Serves 6.*

Party Zest Salad
The What
2 cups diced cooked potatoes
½ cup chopped celery
2 tbsps. instant onion
½ cup diced apple
½ cup dairy sour cream
2 tsps. dill flakes
½ tsp. salt
¼ tsp. pepper
paprika
¼ cup Sauterne

The How
Toss all ingredients except paprika together. Hold chilled,

tossing together a few times. Dust with paprika and serve.

Sherry-Bean Bake
The What
1 can (28 ozs.) baked beans
⅓ cup medium sherry
½ tsp. dry mustard
1 tsp. instant coffee powder
2 tbsps. brown sugar
2 tbsps. lemon juice

The How
Mix all ingredients well. Bake in individual beanpots at 350° for 30 minutes. *Serves 4.*

White Wine Sauce
For fish or vegetables.

The What
3 ozs. Sauterne or Chablis
1 tbsp. instant onion
¼ cup sliced carrot
1 bay leaf
thin peel of 1 lemon
1 tsp. parsley flakes
1 egg, lightly beaten

The How
Simmer all ingredients except egg until liquid is reduced by half. Mix with egg and add to 1 cup medium white sauce. Reheat just below boil and serve.

Spiceburg Sauce
For apple pie.

The What
½ cup Burgundy
½ cup red cinnamon candies
1 tbsp. grated lemon peel
1 pinch salt

The How
Heat wine to simmer. Add cinnamon candies. Stir until dissolved. Add lemon peel and simmer a minute or two. Hold hot until serving over warm apple pie. *Serves 6.*

CHOOSING AND STORING WINE

The best rule in wine buying is to buy what you like. First you will want to get acquainted with the five main types of wine—white table wine, red table wine, appetizer wine, sparkling wine, and dessert wine—and then you can experiment until you know your favorites. A representative starter assortment might be three red table wines —a mellow red, a Burgundy, and a Zinfandel; three whites —such as a Sauterne, a Chablis, and a Riesling; a vin Rosé— —perhaps a Grenache; a bottle of dry or medium dry Sherry, and one of Port; a dry and a sweet Vermouth; and a bottle of Champagne.

Now you can find out what you like in different types and price ranges. You may find that stocking to your taste is not at all expensive. Once you have a dozen or so bottles at home, you have to store them.

Wine can be kept for long periods in a cool area that is not brightly lighted. Store where direct sun rays can never strike the bottles. Wines that are corked must be stored on their sides to keep the corks from drying out. Temperature should not be above 70°F. Wines with metal screw caps or plastic corks may be stored in any position. Wine can be refrigerated for weeks with no ill effects. Once opened, all wines should be reclosed and refrigerated. Because of their high alcohol content, dessert and appetizer wines keep well for a month or more after being opened.

SERVING WINES

Some people serve wine by ritual, others just open the bottle and pass it along like the meat and vegetable dishes. Ritually, you open a red wine two hours before serving, to let it breathe. Pull the cork gently so you do not disturb the wine. White wine may be opened and kept in a bucket of ice on the side table.

Generally speaking, red wines should be served at a temperature of 60 to 70°F., white wines at a temperature between 45 and 55°F., and dessert wines at room temperature. The trend, however, is changing. The majority now prefer chilled sherry and vermouth when drinking them before dinner. Some even serve them "on the rocks," a practice that causes traditional wine bibbers to shudder. However, if you like your appetizer wines chilled, we see no reason to criticize.

A good all-purpose glass is a stemmed, clear glass of 6- to 9-ounce capacity. This allows room for the fragrance to collect above the wine. Serving for appetizer wines is 2 to 3 ounces, and for table and sparkling wines 4 to 5 ounces.

WINES AND FOODS

Part of your enjoyment of wines lies in sampling and comparing to discover which you like the best. Generally speaking, drier types are served as appetizers and with meals, and sweeter wines with desserts. However, even the experts admit there are no hard-and-fast rules, so be guided by your own personal taste.

Class	Types	When and with What
APPETIZER WINES	Sherry Vermouth Flavored wines	Serve chilled, without food, or with hors d'oeuvres, nuts, or cheese.
WHITE TABLE WINES	SAUTERNE Semillon Sauvignon Blanc CHABLIS Chenin Blanc Pinot Blanc RHINE WINE Sylvaner Riesling Traminer	Serve, chilled, with lighter dishes: chicken, fish, omelets, or any white meat.
RED TABLE WINES	BURGUNDY Gamay Red Pinot Pinot Noir CHIANTI CLARET Grignolino Cabernet Zinfandel ROSÉ	Serve with hearty dishes (at about 60° to 65°): steaks, game, roasts, chops, cheese dishes, spaghetti. Rosé goes with almost any food.
DESSERT WINES	Muscatel Angelica Cream Sherry Tokay Port	Serve chilled or cool with fruits, cookies, cheese, cake, or nuts.

SPARKLING WINES	CHAMPAGNE Brut (very dry) Sec (semi-dry) Doux (sweet) Pink Champagne Sparkling Burgundy	Serve well chilled with any food to those who like sparkling wine. Very good in party punches.

9. The Art of Seasoning

The first step to gourmet cooking is learning about herbs and spices and their uses.

Spices and herbs are intended to accent, not submerge, the flavor of fine foods. Until you acquire skill and knowledge, caution in quantity is the word. If in doubt about the strength of a spice, roll and crush it with your finger tips, then inhale the aroma. Taste it delicately with the tip of your tongue. The strength will be evident and can guide you in the use of this particular spice. Since no two palates are the same, it is better to under-season than to over-season.

Spices and herbs should be stored in the coolest part of the kitchen and tightly sealed to prevent loss of the aromatic oils that contain the flavor. Get into the habit of using one or two every day. You will enjoy your meals more and more.

Herb Directory	Appetizers	Soups	Fish	Eggs and Cheese	Meats
BASIL	Vegetable juices Tomatoes Sea Food	Minestrone Turtle Broiled toppings	Shrimp Sole Broiled fish	Rarebit Scrambled eggs	Lamb Liver Sausage
BAY LEAF	Aspics Kabobs	Stocks Bouquet garni	Court bouillon Fish kabobs	Scrambled eggs Cream cheese	Stews Pot roasts Marinades
CHERVIL	Garnish	Spinach	Fish butter sauces	Egg omelets	Veal Beef
MARJORAM	Mushrooms Pâtés	Clam Turtle Onion	Broiled Baked	Omelets Scrambled	Pork Veal Lamb Beef
MINT	Fruit cup Fruit juice	Pea		Cream cheese	Lamb Veal
OREGANO	Tomatoes	Minestrone Tomato Bean	Stuffing		Pork Lamb Sausage Meat sauce
PARSLEY	Garnish Canapés	Garnish Bouquet garni Chowder	All fish Court bouillon	Omelets Scrambled	Lamb Veal Stews Steak

Herb Directory	Appetizers	Soups	Fish	Eggs and Cheese	Meats
ROSEMARY	Turtle pâté Fruit cup	Turtle Spinach Pea Chicken	Salmon Stuffing	Omelets Scrambled	Ragouts Meat sauce Ham loaf Beef stew
SAGE	Cottage and Cheddar cheeses	Chowder Creamed soups	Stuffing	Cottage Cheddar	Pork Sausage Stews Stuffings
SAVORY	Vegetable juices	Fish Consommé Bean	Broiled Baked	Deviled Scrambled	Pork Veal
TARRAGON	Fruit Tomatoes Seafood	Tomato Consommé Turtle Chicken	Frog's Legs Broiled lobster and other fish	All eggs	Sweetbreads Veal Yorkshire pudding
THYME	Seafood Tomatoes Chowders	Borscht Gumbo Vegetable	Broiled Baked	Shirred eggs Cottage cheese	Mutton Veal

Herb Directory	Poultry and Game	Vegetables	Salads	Sauces	Desserts
BASIL	Venison Duck	Tomatoes Eggplant Onions	Green Tomato Fish Butter sauces	Spaghetti Orange	Fruit compote
BAY LEAF	Stew Pies	Carrots Tomatoes Potatoes	Seafood Aspics	Marinades Espagnole Champagne	
CHERVIL	Chicken Butter sauce		Green	Madeira Bearnaise Vinaigrette	
MARJORAM	Chicken and Goose Dressings	Carrots Peas Spinach	Green Chicken	Brown Sour Cream	
MINT		Carrots New Potatoes Zucchini	Fruit Cole slaw Green	Mint	Frostings Fruit Ices
OREGANO	Stuffings Marinades Pheasant Guinea hen	Tomatoes Cabbage Broccoli Lentils	Seafood Aspic	Spaghetti Tomato	
PARSLEY	Bouquet garni Stuffing	Potatoes Carrots Peas	Fish Potato Green	Beurre Noir Bordelaise Tartare	

Herb Directory	Poultry and Game	Vegetables	Salads	Sauces	Desserts
ROSEMARY	Capon Duck Partridge Rabbit	Peas Spinach	Fruit		Fruit
SAGE	All stuffings	Limas Eggplant Onions Tomatoes			
SAVORY	Chicken stuffings	Beans Rice Sauerkraut	Green Russian	Fish sauce Horseradish	Pear compote
TARRAGON	Duck Chicken and mushrooms Squab	Salsify Celery Mushroom	Green Fish Chicken	Bearnaise Tartare Mustard	
THYME	All stuffings	Onions Carrots Beets	Pickled beets Aspics	Creole Espagnole Garni	

Index

Appetizers and Dips

Barbecue dip, 87
Beer dip, 84
Blue cheese dip, 84
Caviar blini, 166
Cheese dip, 83
Chicken liver dip, 85
Clam dip, 84
Fondue Swiss, 121, 168
Guacamole dip, 85
Ham cornets, 167
Ham dip, 86
Hickory cheese dip, 87
Instant onion dip, 86
Lobster en croute, 164
Pâté maison, 165
Quiche Lorraine, 164

Baby Foods

Baby dinner de luxe, 160
Blended fruits, 160
Chicken for baby, 162
Liver dinner, 162
Meat and vegetable dinner, 162
Vegetables for baby, 161

Beef and Veal Dishes

Beef and olive casserole, 46
Beef rolls, 95

Beef tongue au gratin, 172
Blackfriars roast, 50
Boeuf à la mode, 175
Boeuf Bourguignon, 177
Braised beef, 174
Burgerole, 36
Burgunchilis, 206
Casserole epicure, 208
Cheeseburger pie, 66
Cheeseburger, sherried, 205
Chili Vinos, 57
Corned beef cones, 111
Honey chili, 52
Jiffy casserole, 62
Lazy shepherd's pie, 67
Meat loaf, 96
Meat sauce and spaghetti, 48
Mock duck, 103
Party steak pot, 202
Pot au feu, 176
Shepherd's pie, 38
Skillet braised beef, 50
Stroganoff, 53, 63, 100
Sweetbreads in Marsala, 173
Tournedos Bearnaise, 177
Veal scallops, 178
Veal steak Parmigiana, 56

Beverages

Alexander, 89
Basic Daiquiri, 90

Coffee tropical, 88
Darwin Daiquiri, 90
Fruit Daiquiri, 90
Grasshopper, 89
Hawaiian Blossom, 91
Mocha float, 88
Orange apricot nectar, 88
Pineapple banana cream, 88
Screwdriver, 89
Stinger, 90
Whiskey sour, 89

Desserts

Blancmange, 154
Caramel-iced cream puffs, 197
Chestnuts in cream, 200
Chocolate Bavarian cream, 153
Chocolate-iced rolls, 198
Cocktail velvet, 157
Coffee-caramel pudding, 198
Crêpes Suzettes Jubilee, 197
Frozen fruit cream, 158
Fruit and ice cream snowball, 199
Instant Charlotte Russe, 156
Instant chocolate sauce, 159
Jellied Irish coffee, 201
Jiffy cheese pie, 158
Lemon sauce, 159
Maple custard, 155
Ocean foam, 157
Orange sauce, 159
Peaches in champagne, 200
Peaches in red wine, 200
Rosy applesauce, 157
Spiceburg apple pie sauce, 209
Strawberry Bavarian, 154
Western apple crisp, 156

Eggs and Cheese

Blender omelet, 119
Blender rarebit, 122
Cheese and bacon puff, 122
Cheese and onion pie, 123
Cheese and rice casserole, 35
Cheese fluff omelet, 121

Cheese fondue, 121
Cheese noodles, 96
Cheese omelet, 120
Creole linguini, 98
Egg and onion casserole, 43
Ham omelet, 120
Herb omelet, 120
Mexican omelet, 120
Quiche Lorraine, 164
Savory poached eggs, 58
Spud 'n cheese, 41, 64
Sunny eye lunch, 61
Swiss scramble, 49
Tummy picnic casserole, 41
Zippy cheese casserole, 97

Fowl

Ceylon chicken pie, 67
Chicken and mushroom casserole, 107
Chicken breasts Italiano, 191
Chicken breasts Vladimir, 44
Chicken croquettes, 105
Chicken curry, 207
Chicken Kiev, 192
Chicken loaf, 106
Chicken in wine sauce, 188
Chicken Oahu, 57
Chicken paprika, 46
Chicken tarragon, 191
Chicken with Lobster, 189
Duckling with orange sauce, 188
Supreme breast of chicken, 190
Turkey casserole, 37
Velvet chicken, 106
Wonder chicken, 112

Ham and Bacon

Cheese 'n bacon, 40
Down country chowder, 68
Festive ham loaf, 111
Glazed ham steak, 54
Ham and rice, 52, 205
Ham soufflé, 101

Ham stuffed peppers, 101
Hoedown chowder, 55
Indian casserole, 37
Jellied ham supreme, 167
Stuffed ham cones, 167

Lamb

Lamb Palermo, 50
Savory Lamb chops, 174

Liver

Loaf, 102
Pâté maison, 165
Veal liver with orange sauce, 172

Sausage and Pork

Corn pudding, 99
Crown jewel pie, 76
Goulash Vienna, 49
Hawaiian sausage, 71
Heaven hash, 72
Hot pot, 75
New England sausage, 54
Polish bigos, 79
Quick sausage casserole, 72, 79, 81
Sausage and sweet potato, 73
Sausage in ale, 75
Sausage-lima casserole, 72
Sausage-stuffed acorn squash, 80
Sausage-stuffed eggplant, 74
Sausage with potato stuffing, 70
Sausage with red beans, 80
Savory kernels, 61
Savory pork casserole, 39
Scalloped sausage with corn, 78
Stuffed peppers, 69
Toss pot, 76
Tummy picnic, 41
Wiener and sauerkraut, 77

Pancakes and Waffles

Basic pancakes, 91
Blueberry pancakes, 94
Caviar blini, 166
Chocolate waffles, 92
Crêpes Suzettes Jubilee, 197
Foolproof popovers, 93
Green corn pancakes, 93
Orange pancakes, 92
Oyster pancakes, 94

Salad Dressings

Artur dressing, 148
Basic French, 145
Blue cheese, 147
Creamy French, 146
Cucumber low-calorie, 150
French fruit, 149
Herbed dressing, 147
Ketchup dressing, 148
Kong Loo dressing, 148
Low-calorie dream, 146
Vinaigrette, 149
Vincenzo dressing, 147

Salads

Ceylon salad, 17
Cottage cheese superba, 151
Deviled egg, 152
Hamlet Salad, 17
Luau salad, 152
Nelson salad, 17
Party zest, 208
Perfection mold, 151
Ruby jewel, 150

Sandwich spreads

Chicken liver, 141
Crabmeat spread, 141
Date-nut spread, 139
Deviled ham paste, 140
Egg spread, 141
Marmalade nut, 140
Mushroom butter, 143
Nut butter, 144
Sardine spread, 143
Shrimp butter, 194

Tuna spread, 142
Watercress butter, 144
Wine party spread, 204
Zippy cheese, 143

Sauces

Aioli, 136
Barbecue, 137
Basic cream sauce, 129
Basting, 137
Bearnaise, 136
Beurre de crevettes, 194
Beurre manie, 195
Beurre vert, 193
Brown sauce, 193
Butter sauce, 133
Cheese sauce, 133
Chicken à la king, 130
Cream cheese sauce, 94
Creole sauce, 131
Curry sauce, mayonnaise, 196
Farmdale chicken, 132
Hollandaise, 135
Honey mayonnaise, 134
Madère sauce, 195
Meat sauce, 138
Mornay sauce, 132, 196
Mushroom, 132, 194
Pesto Italiano, 138
Poulette sauce, 131
Provençale sauce, 195
Tartare sauce, 136
Thousand Island, 135
Waterfowl sauce, 133
White wine sauce, 209
Zip sauce, 130

Sea Food

Anchovy-potato pudding, 47
Baked fish tartare, 204
Blue trout in aspic, 181
Bouillabaisse, 180
Butter trout, 182
Crab mousse Marsala, 109
Crab with rice, 166
Curried shrimp, 183
Curried shrimp Ceylon, 104
Filet of sole Amandine, 179
Fish Fillets Marseille, 103
Fish in celery sauce, 44
Fish stick medley, 40
Frog's legs, 182
King crab devils, 105
Lobster Armoricaine, 178
Lobster 'n rice, 33
Lobster turnover, 167
Oysters with spinach, 181
Salmon noodle, 32
Scampi Chablis, 207
Scampi Moderne, 184
Scampi piquant, 51
Shore society mold, 108
Spaghetti and clam, 53
Tuna party mold, 109
Tuna puffs, 65

Soups

Beef and mushroom broth, 169
Borscht in a hurry, 113
Clam and chicken broth, 169
Clam bisque, 114
Cold chicken curry, 116
Cream of cauliflower, 170
Cream of lima bean, 118
Cream of spinach, 170
Curried chicken cream, 171
Elite cream of mushroom, 115
Five minute soup, 60
Golden cheese soup, 203
Green pea supreme, 117
Leftover bean soup, 117
Louisiana bisque, 118
Minestrone, 116
Onion soup, 168
Oyster bisque, 117
Quick cheese soup, 114
Sherried green pea soup, 203
Shrimp and lobster soup, 171
Vichysoisse, 113

Index

Spaghetti and Other Pastas

Creole linguini, 98
One-dish casserole dinner, 48
Skillet lasagna, 55
Spaghetti and meat sauce, 48
Spaghetti, skillet, 48
Spaghetti 'n clam, 53

Toppings

Beet salad, 15
Ceylon salad, 17
Cucumber and onion, 16
Curry mayonnaise, 16
Egg strips, 17
Fleurette, 15
Fried apple slices, 17
Hamlet salad, 17
Horseradish cream, 16
Nelson salad, 17
Red meat jelly, 15

Vegetables

Artichokes maitre d'hotel, 187
Asparagus vinaigrette, 186
Calico bean, 35
Cornfield casserole, 128
Corn fritters, 124
Corn pie, 126
Corn pudding, 99
Creamed spinach, 185
Creamy beany casserole, 33
Crunchy au gratin, 63
Green rice, 185
Instant potato salad, 64
Jiffy casserole, 62
Little peas, Robert, 184
Mixed vegetable casserole, 34
Onion custard, 42
Potatoes Florentine, 65
Potatoes Grillées, 59
Potato pudding, 124
Potatoes western, 62
Potatoes with caviar, 187
Puffed spud casserole, 126
Rice and lima casserole, 126
Savory kernels, 61
Sherried bean bake, 209
Sherried mushrooms, 186
Spanish rice ring, 125
Spinach timbales, 98
Stuffed eggplant, 74
Stuffed peppers, 69, 101
Sunny eye lunch, 61
Sweet potato poem, 125
Vegetable custard, 127
Zingy beets, 127